American Journey of George W. Strong

by
Peter S. Centa

Bloomington, IN  Milton Keynes, UK
authorHOUSE®

AuthorHouse™
1663 Liberty Drive, Suite 200
Bloomington, IN 47403
www.authorhouse.com
Phone: 1-800-839-8640

AuthorHouse™ UK Ltd.
500 Avebury Boulevard
Central Milton Keynes, MK9 2BE
www.authorhouse.co.uk
Phone: 08001974150

First published by AuthorHouse 12/29/2006

ISBN: 978-1-4259-7296-7 (sc)
ISBN: 978-1-4259-7297-4 (hc)

Library of Congress Control Number: 2006909259

Printed in the United States of America
Bloomington, Indiana

This book is printed on acid-free paper.

"My name is Ozymandias, king of kings;
Look on my works, ye mighty, and despair!"
Nothing beside remains. Round the decay
Of that colossal wreck, boundless and bare,
The lone and level sands strech far away.

Percy Bysshe Shelley (1792-1822)

In Memory of the many brave men and women who have passed and made America the great country that it would become and **in recognition of** the persons and institutions that preserve their legacy without whose help this book would not be possible.

Preface

The past for many Americans may be ten, thirty or fifty years ago. In some cases the distant past dates back to World War II or the Great Depression. When looking beyond the turn of the century to the 1800's, knowledge of the lives and contributions of pioneer Americans in many cases has been long forgotten. Accounts of their heroic deeds and inspiring convictions lie buried in museums, archives and libraries across the country. Historical research often result in the realization that our lifestyle today is in someway attributed to the difficult journey of those who passed before us. The life of George W. Strong is symbolic of that journey and spirit which established the towns and cities in a newly discovered wilderness that was earlier America.

This fictional biography is not meant to be the accurate personal profile of a man that was born over two hundred years ago. His private thoughts, his relationship with his family and friends, his religious convictions and his perspective on wealth and power will never be truly known. One can only attempt to perceive what the personality of this early American may have been based on limited documentation and his involvement in actual events.

There is a brief references to many historic events covering centuries. Time and again it was the past that influenced the destiny of the Strongs and finally George W. Strong. Information from books, newspapers, census data and early records of towns in America contribute to the background surrounding the life of this pioneer. His name and that of his ancestors is often mentioned. The pages of history expose a hard life for Strong and his ancestors by today's standard. This biography is also a reminder that in some cases a tragic and sorrowful ending was part of the early American legacy.

The purpose of the biography is to remind us that there were many inspiring Americans living in the eighteenth and nineteenth centuries and their spirit and accomplishments should not be forgotten. Often times we need not look beyond our village, town or city to uncover the contribution of one of these great Americans who by now is all but forgotten.

Contents - Footnotes

Information on George Strong taken from
Wing, Talcott E., *History of Monroe County,
Michigan*

3   *The Lure of Frenchtown*

Information on history of Monroe taken from
Bulkley, John, *History of Monroe County,
Michigan* Vol. I and II

Information on history of Monroe taken from
Wing, Talcott E., *History of Monroe County, Michigan*

The early newspapers of Monroe from 1828 to 1836
were the *Michigan Sentinel* and the *Gazette*

The newspaper became the *Advocate* until 1839.
It was followed by the *Commercial* until 1856.
The early newspapers were the source for much of
the early information on George W. Strong and the
city of Monroe.

6 Family Life and Hannah Strong

7 A Time for Buildings

8 Tragedy

Reference for the Battle of Shiloh from Internet
"http://www.civilwarhome.com/shiloh.htm" and
"www.civilwarhhome.com/sholohdescription.htm"

9 Final Years of the Strong Hotel

10 Final Years of the George W. Strong

Bibliography

Below are listed the sources and others credited in the text whose help is much appreciated.

Dwight, Benjamin W. *Dwight's History of the Strong Family,* Originally published, Albany, New York, 1871 - Reprinted, Baltimore. Maryland 1975, 1984, 2000 Volume I & II

Lamour Printing Company - *Pageant of Historic Monroe 1929*

LaVoy, Lambert M. Bay. Settlement of Monroe County, Michigan Copyright 1971 by Lambert M. Lavoy - second printing, 1972

McNutly, Marjorie Grant, *Glastonbury: From Settlement to Suburb*, The Historical Society of Glastonbury, 1995 - Copyright 1975 expanded edition 1995

Potinaro, Pierluigi and knirsch, Franko, *The Cartography of North America 1500 - 1800* Facts of File, Inc. 460 Park Avenue South, New York 10016 - A Bishop Book

Roberts, Gary Boyd & Reitwiesner, William Addams *American Ancestors and Cousins of the Princess of Wales* - Genealogical Publishing Co., Inc Baltimore, 1985 Copyright 1984 by Genealogical Publishing Co., Ind.

Vollrath J. A., Monroe Piers, Compiled and Published by the Monroe County Library System -3700 South Custer Rd. Monroe, Mich.

Wing, Talcott E. History of Monroe County Michigan - Illustrated New York: Munsell & Company, Publishers. 1890

Kohrman, David Images of America Kalamazoo, Michigan Arcadia Publishing, an imprint of Tempus Publishing

Chapter 1 - **The Pioneers -God and the land**

Four hundred years is a blink in time when referring to recorded human history. That is how long it took for America to become the great country it is today. Every city in early America started in the same manner. A few pioneers, some leaders, some followers built settlements, villages, towns, and then cities guided by the rules of a representative republic. A few settlements remained crossroads on the highways of America while others would be numbered among the largest cities in the world. Lost in every town in America is the story of great Americans. There are those who discovered the land along with those who tamed the land. Forgotten with each achievement are the names - names of those persons who rest in the museums and archives of every city and town waiting to be remembered once again. The western end of Lake Erie in southeastern Michigan was one location in early America where a pioneer hero was rediscovered. The contribution of George W. Strong to Monroe, Michigan, took place from 1832 to 1892 and is all but forgotten now. Thanks to those who preserve historical information and the fact that there is always someone interested in the past of our great country, his story and that of his ancestors can be revived. Among the early records of the Strong family are the names of Simon Strong of Cambridgeshire in 1273; Joscelin and William le Strong at about the same time; Hugo Strong of Yorkshire in the reign of King Henry V; John Strong of Suffolk and Norfok in 1378; Peter, son of Martyn Strong of London, in 1539; Nicolas Strong of Dublin, Ireland, in 1634, and the Reverend William Strong of Dorsetshire, noted preacher at Westminster Abbey in the first half of the seventeenth century.

It is said that one member of the Shropshire (Salop) line of the family married a Welsh heiress and made his home in the country of Caernarvon. This Strong is said to be the one Richard Strong of that country who moved to Taunton, in the county of Somerset, England, in the latter part of the sixteenth century.

A chain of events was set in motion in England that would bring the Strong family and those seeking religious freedom to the colonies across the Atlantic. The Protestant Reformation had torn apart Europe beginning with Martin Luther (1483 - 1546). The reformation took a much different form in England as the monarchy passed from one religion to another. King Henry VIII wanted his marriage to Catherine of Aragon annulled by the pope so that he could marry Ann Boleyn. Circumstances were working against him. Annulling the marriage would signify that the first papal dispensation to Catherine was in error, something the pope was not willing to admit. Henry VIII was sympathetic to the views of Martin Luther, who gave the king some radical ideas, thanks to his advisors. The English church then split from the Roman Catholic Church and the King became the leader of the Church of England and could grant himself an annulment.

The Strongs living at the time of Henry VIII were Catholic peasants. They lived in the villages outside the larger cities. Like their name, they were known for their physical and mental strength. Their peasant lifestyle included bread, cheese, beer and what their land could provide. The Strong men were blessed with long life and many children. The religious changes of the time were taking place among the royalty, but were beginning to be discussed by the peasants, as well as the Strongs.

Edward VI, following Henry, turned the Church of England into a Protestant church. Queen Mary (Bloody Mary) who was raised in France was the next monarch and tried to make the country Catholic again, executing a number of Protestants in the process. Mary died after five years and might have reversed the trend to Catholicism if she had lived longer. Mary was succeeded by Elizabeth (The Virgin Queen) who was the daughter of Ann Boleyn. She assumed the throne in 1558 and reigned until 1603. Elizabeth understood that her country was being torn apart by the warring doctrines. While she repealed Mary's Catholic legislation, she did not return to Edward's more austere Protestantism. Rather, she worked out a compromise church that retained as much of the Catholic church as possible while putting into place most of the foundational ideas of Protestantism.

Religion was not the only change taking place in England. Money was introduced, replacing the barter system. Commerce and shipbuilding were increasing and new thinkers were making their ideas known. More important, printed information was changing the culture of England. Jonathon Gutenberg (1395 - 1468) with his invention of the printing press had one of the greatest impacts on modern history. His invention marked the beginning of the information age and a Bible in the vernacular was available to the masses. The Reformation with all its twists and turns was aided by the availability of information.

The generations of Strongs living under the various Monarchs also began to change as England was changing. Upon the death of Queen Elizabeth, James VI, King of Scots (son of Mary, Queen of Scots), succeeded as James I, King of England, thereupon uniting the crowns but not the governments of England and Scotland. King James is most remembered for having the Bible translated into the King James Version.

A change followed not only with the monarchy of England but also with the religious convictions of the Strongs. The peasant class was by far the largest among the population of England. Many were literate and were well aware of the changing times. The Strongs were no longer the traditional Catholics of the old church, but were now torn between the Church of England and the new information being preached on the Reformation. Most notably, the Puritan ideas were gaining wide interest as an alternative to established religion. With learning and intellectual maturity came the driving desire for religious freedom.

Living during the time of King James were George Strong, a tailor, Thomas, Walter, William, Maria, Elizabeth, Richard and more notably, John Strong whose descendant would one day be George Strong, a pioneer father of Monroe, Michigan. John was born about 1610 and was raised in Chard, Somerset, England. His father, Richard, a Catholic, died when John was about five years old. Little is known about John's mother and father because they were commoners. John was raised without the influence of a father and sought his own way at an early age. As a youth, he was introduced to and influenced by the Puritans. For some years, this new religious denomination had been emerging from the struggle between Catholicism and the Reformation for control over the Church of England. The reform movement that emerged was aimed to simplify or *purify* (hence the title "Puritan") the practice of religion within the Protestant church by eliminating the hierarchy and doctrine. Puritan parishioners intended to practice morality and their faith after prayerful reading of the Bible, without reference to any bishop or catechism. For many years the Puritans had suffered more or less persecution depending on the monarch, but continued to prosper and grow in numbers. In 1630, Charles I became embroiled in a nineteen year long struggle leading to civil war. The scene was set for mass migration to the new world.

A related group, the Pilgrims, had settled the first successful English colony in America at Plymouth in 1620. The first Puritan colony in America was established at Salem in 1627, mostly by fishermen who left their families in England. Meanwhile, the Reverend John White, pastor of the Dorchester Parish in England, began the recruitment of families and single young men for the settlement of Puritan colonies in America. His was to be the largest role in the Puritan movement to New England, but he never went there himself. In spite of his disgust at the Kings' meddling with Parliament and the Church, he remained a loyal pastor of the Church of England, but as a Puritan reformer. About 1,000 emigrants sailed in fourteen ships that journeyed to towns around the mouth of the Charles River in 1630. One of the ships was the *Mary and John* which brought about 400 settlers near where the town of Dorchester is located.

First generation in America - John Strong

John Strong was among the many that were influenced by Pastor John White. The Puritan beliefs and the lure of the new land followed him into adulthood as he learned the trade of tanner from William Coogan. At 20 years of age, John married Margery Deane. They had two children, a son, John, and a second child while in England.

John Strong was motivated by his desire for land, which was unobtainable for most in England but easily available in the Massachusetts Colony. In New England, he could also escape a stifling class society of English lords, ladies and clergy. Opportunities were nonexistent for the middle and lower classes. He and his family left England for the new world in 1630 to begin the heritage of the Strongs in America.

The only details of the new land across the ocean was a map made from information Sir Francis Drake and other explorers furnished with names and locations, including Hudson Bay, Cape Cod, James Bay and the Hudson River. The coast that was later known as California was shown for the first time.

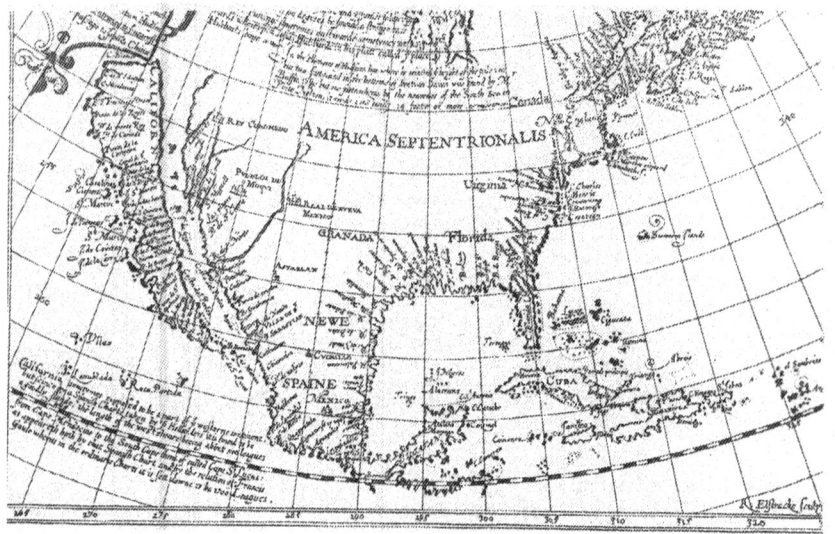

Early map of New World

The following is taken from "Dwight's History of the Strong Family" which consists of two volumes and 1,586 pages.

'The History of the Descendants of Elder John Strong of Northampton, Ct. by Benjamin W. Dwight.

The Strong Family of England was originally located in the county of Shropshire. One of the family married an heiress of Griffith, of the county of Caernarvon, Wales, and went thither to reside in 1545. Richard Strong was of this branch of the family, and was born in the county of Caernarvon in 1561. In 1590 he removed to Taunton, Somersetshire, England, where he died in 1613, leaving a son John then eight years of age, and a daughter Eleanor. ... John Strong was born in Taunton, Eng., in 1605, when he removed to London and afterwards to Plymouth. Having strong Puritan sympathies he sailed from Plymouth for the new world, March 20, 1630, in company with 140 persons, and among them Rev. Messrs. John Warham and John Maverick and Messrs. John Mason and Roger Clapp, in the ship Mary and John (Capt. Squeb) and arrived at Nantucket, Mass. (Hull), about twelve miles southeast from Boston, after a passage of more than seventy days in length, on Sunday, May 30, 1630. ... After searching for a few days, for a good place in which to settle and make homes for themselves, they decided upon the spot, which they called Dorchester, in memory of the endeared home in England.

The voyage across the ocean for John Strong took about 70 days aboard the *Mary and John* under the command of Captain Spueb. The Puritans arrived at Nantasket, Massachusetts about 12 miles southeast of Boston on Sunday, May 30, 1630. The original destination of the vessel was the Charles River but an unfortunate misunderstanding arose between the captain and the passengers which resulted in their being put ashore at Nantasket. After searching for a few days for a place to settle and make a home, John decided on a spot called Dorchester. The wife and one child of John Strong died shortly after landing and John needed help with his baby son, John. Twelve miles northwest of Dorchester in Hingman there was a sixteen year old daughter of Thomas Ford named Abigail. The two had arrived aboard the *Mary and John* with John and his family. John and Abigail soon married.

After helping to establish the town of Dorchester, John Strong moved to Hingham, Massachusetts and on March 9, 1636, took the freeman's oath at Boston. A son, Jedediah, was born in 1637. His stay at Hingham was short because he inherited property in Taunton, Massachusetts in 1638. The family then moved 26 miles southwest to this settlement. Early Puritan practice was harsh for John and Abigail. The practice evolved into Congregationalism. A Code of Law ("Body of Liberties") was enacted in Massachusetts in 1641. At about the same time, a law was passed to limit the practice of religion to that which the Pilgrims and Puritans observed. This was thought to be a setback for religious freedom. While at Taunton, he was deputy to the general court in Plymouth from 1641 to 1643. John and Abigail remained in Taunton until 1645. During this period six children were born.

Abigail Strong's father moves to Connecticut

The year 1639 was the last of the boom years for English settlement by Puritans. In 1640, Charles I was under attack by the Scots as well as by several English factions. He didn't have time to oppress his subjects anymore and so emigration ebbed. Massachusetts and Connecticut began to see a recession in land value. As a result, John Strong had the distinction of being among the first families in the New England Colonies.

Many of the early emigrants had come expecting to convert the natives to Christianity. But conversion efforts failed from the beginning. The settlers' relationship with the Indians was also stormy, which forced Strong and many of the settlers to seek safety from the Indians. Chickenpox and smallpox soon decimated the Indians, causing them to vacate large areas. The settlers promptly occupied some of these areas. The growing population brought distress to the early settlers around the Bay. The soil there was rocky and infertile. They didn't have enough land to share with the newcomers. Their livestock had multiplied and grazing land was insufficient.

About half of the first settlers in Dorchester, including Abigail Strong's father and family, elected to move overland to the banks of the Connecticut River in 1635 where there were a few settlers already and plenty of fertile soil. The location at Matianuck became known as Windsor, Connecticut. Other settlers occupied Hartford and Wethersfield, Connecticut. The three towns together founded Connecticut Colony with its capitol at Hartford.

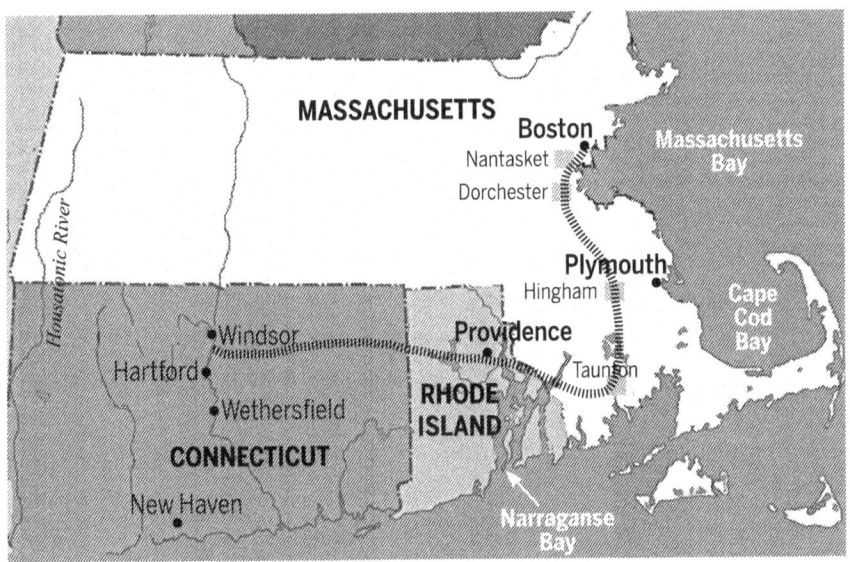

John Strong travels West

John Strong and Abigail later followed in 1645. A tanning business was started anew and a home was built on what is now known as the Deacon Jasper Morgan place. Abigail and John Strong added six more children to their family while at Windsor. John's first son (also John) by his first wife survived to found his particular branch of the Strong family.

Citizens were assigned duties in the management of the town's business. John was in charge of cow breeding. The Ford and the Strong families were never able to settle into a comfortable routine while in Windsor because of the conflicts not only with the Indians, but also because of European wars with the Dutch on the Hudson River Valley and the French from the Saint Lawrence River Valley. As early as 1632, each settlement had its contingent of militia. Men between the ages of sixteen and sixty drilled for one day each month. All men were required to maintain arms and sufficient ammunition. Mounted men were gathered into a troop on horseback. Large portions of every town were enclosed in defensive palisades.

The first military test took place after the arrival of Abigail's father and ended as John Strong and Abigail arrived at Windsor. A fierce tribe, the Pequot, and their Indian allies from coastal lands east of the Connecticut Valley began to attack the settlement. In reprisal to killings and torture, Connecticut declared war on the Pequot in 1637. Each of the three towns provided thirty men and John Mason from Windsor was made the commander. Moving east from the Connecticut River, Captain Mason and his force found the Pequot encamped within a large palisade atop a bluff where Mystic, Connecticut is located today. The Connecticut force already was supported by sixty Mohegan who had no love for the Pequot. Wanting to improve his odds, Captain Mason moved his force farther east where he enlisted about two hundred Narragansett warriors. Early one morning after "yielding themselves up to God" the English attacked the Pequot from two directions. The friendly Indian forces followed. The Pequot were caught napping. Captain Mason charged first, taking one arrow in his helmet and one in his quilted jacket before other of his forces could join him. They charged down an alley between the tents and Mason killed about seven Indians using musket and sword with only a little help. The space between the wigwams was so restricted that the English could not use swords or muskets well. Mason then grabbed a torch and set fire to the thatch that covered every wigwam and within just a few minutes the Pequot fort and its contents were burned to the ground. The English left the fort and picked off the Pequot who tried to escape. The Mohegan and Narragansett aided in eliminating the threat from the Pequot and the settlers began to enjoy a calmer time.

Just as family life began to settle, John and Abigail were faced with a different type of family crisis. In 1651, a Sumptuary Law was passed forbidding the wearing of gold, silver, silk hoods or scarves and ribbons, but the law did not apply to any magistrate or public officer; their wives and children were also excluded. To the dismay of John and Abigail Strong, two of their own daughters were accused of "sumptuous" conduct. The girls were reprimanded and fined. They were ordered to follow the strict Puritan dress code.

The girls had been influenced by news of a Puritan preacher in Salem who had some new, but not so popular, ideas for many. Roger Williams became popular in the early 1630s when he preached two ideas that Puritan leaders did not like. First, he believed that the

Indians owned the land where the Massachusetts Bay Colony was founded. Second and more important to the Strong girls, he preached that every person had the right to worship God in his or her own way. The girls thought what they wore should not reflect how they worshiped. The Puritan leaders were wrong, Williams said, to force everyone in the colony to worship God according to Puritan rules. With his second point, Williams touched on another important idea in American democracy: the belief in religious liberty or freedom of religion.

John Strong elected Ruling Elder

Farther northwest on the Connecticut River, the tiny settlement at Northampton was declining. The town needed more people, especially skilled workmen. The five settlers there offered forty acres to any skilled worker who would join them. John answered the call in 1659, leaving sons John Jr. and Return in Windsor to continue the tanning business there. John bought land at the northeast corner of what is now Main and South Street for his tannery, later occupied by the Northampton Hotel. Across Main Street at South Street, on about an acre of land, he established his home. This land would remain in the Strong family for three generations. He and his family farmed about forty acres of land on the flood plain, his booty for coming to Northampton. They and the community soon prospered. John Strong helped found First Church of Lebanon in 1661. Two years later he was elected the ruling Elder of the Church. This resulted in the historic reference to him as **Elder John Strong**. His importance to the community grew, and the contributions of John and his children included support of Harvard University.

Later, while at Northampton, Elder John and Abigail had reason to continue fearing for their safety. Northampton's original settlers, so they thought, had purchased nine square miles of land for one hundred fathoms (one fathom equals six feet) of wampum, several gifts, including a woman, and the plowing of sixteen acres of land. Unfortunately, the Nonotusk Indians felt that they had allowed the settlers only shared use of the land and that they had retained all their former rights to the land. This led to friction between the

Northampton settlers and their Indian neighbors. The son of Chief Massasoit of the Wamponoeg tribe, thinking that the colonists would eventually evict the tribe from all its land, assumed the title of "King Philip" and mobilized other tribes. In 1675, they began what became known as "King Philip's War" and set out to massacre all white settlers in New England. Thirty towns were attacked; several were destroyed.

The Indians began the war from their safe place in a swamp west of what is now Rhode Island. Militia contingents from Boston, Plymouth and Connecticut were mobilized to rendezvous there during a cold December day. After sleeping out on the frozen ground, they marched fifteen miles into the swamp; fortunately, the mud had frozen. They found a four acre Indian camp heavily fortified with thicket, a high palisade and blockhouses for crossfire. A thousand English soldiers stormed the fort, putting it to the torch like the Mystic tactic forty years earlier. All the Indian men, women and children were killed except for a few who escaped into the swamp. King Philip was assassinated by a traitor Indian employed by the Colonial troops, but the war dragged on for two years. Northampton was attacked in March of 1676; the Indians broke through the fort and killed some of the settlers. Elder John Strong's infant granddaughter, Sarah, was killed by Indians. One tenth of all white male settlers were killed during King Philip's War.

Death of Abigail and Elder John Strong

The difficult pioneer life first took its toll on Abigail. Having lived in log cabins, moving three times and bearing 16 children, Abigail died in 1688 at the age of 74. This Colonial New England Strong family, combined with those of the sixteen children from Elder John and Abigail, was the source of the tens of thousands of Strong descendants in North America. The youngest child, Jedediah, the ancestor of George W. Strong, farmed Elder John's land. When Elder John was 77 years old, he deeded his tanning business to his son, Ebenezer. In later years his son, Samuel, moved into the house with his family to help care for him. Elder John Strong died April 14, 1699, at the age of 94.

John signed his will by mark. It provided for all his children but evened up amounts by taking bills from those children he had earlier helped beyond their share. A full share was about forty pounds. Sons Samuel and Jerijah were excused from the will.

He served as deputy to the General Court in Plymouth from 1641 to 1644. In 1645 removing to Windsor, Ct. he was appointed with four others, Capt John Mason, Roger Ludlow, Henry Wolcott and Israel Stoughton, all very leading men in the infant colony 'to superintend and bring forward the settlement of that place', which had been settled in 1636 by a portion of the same colony that with him had founded Dorchester. In 1659, John Strong removed from Windsor to Northampton, Mass, of which he was one of the first and most active founders. He continued to reside in Northampton for forty years and was a leading man in the affairs of the town and the church. He was a tanner and very prosperous in his business. John Strong was most usually referred to in the early days of Northampton, as Elder John Strong. How he obtained his office and this title appears in the following quotation from the church records in Northampton. 'After solemn and extraordinary seeking to God for his direction and blessing, the church chose John Strong first ruling Elder. He was ordained June 24, 1663, 'by the imposition of the hands of the pastor, Rev. Eleazar Mather.'

The eldest and youngest children of John and Abigail were 32 years apart in age. His wife Abigail was about 16 years of age at her marriage in 1630, at which time John was about 25. She died July 6, 1688 at the age of 74. He died April 14, 1699 at the age of 94.

This letter written in a clear, fair hand, was in Jan. 1871, in the possession of Learned Hebard, Esp., of Lebanon, Ct., where it was read by Benjamin W. Dwight and placed in Volume II of "Dwight's History of the Strong Family".

The great numbers of Strong descendants are primarily descendants of three of the sixteen children that lived to establish families of their own: Thomas, Jedediah and Ebenezer. Thomas, the first child, lived to be 56. Jedediah lived to age 96, and Ebenezer lived to age

86. George W. Strong of Monroe, Michigan, was a descendant of the Jedediah line.

Second Generation in America
Jedediah Strong (1637-1733)

One of the children of John and Abigail was Jedediah who was born in 1637 in Connecticut. He was first married in November 1662, to Freedom Woodward, then to Abigail Stebbins in 1681 and for a third time to Mary (Hart) Lee before he died in 1733. Jedediah had 9 children who survived beyond infancy. His first wife, FreedomWoodard, was born in 1642 at Dorchester, Massachusetts, the daughter of Henry Woodward who came to the colonies from England and who was a noted member of the Dorchester church. The family later moved to Northampton, Connecticut, in 1659 where Henry was killed by lightning at the upper corn mill in 1683. He was licensed to order and sell wines and liquors for several years, as reputable then as any other business.

Jedediah was a farmer at Northampton until 1709, when at the age of 70 years he moved with his family to Coventry, Connecticut, where 24 years later he died in 1733 at the age of 96. During the years 1677-1699, he was paid 18 shillings a year for blowing the trumpet on Sunday to summon the people to church. His wife, Freedom, died in 1681 and he married the same year to Abigail Stebbens, born in 1660. Abigail died in 1689 and Jedediah married for the third time in 1689 to Mrs. Mary (Hart) Lee, widow of John Lee. He lived with his first wife nineteen years, his second seven years, and the third nine years. Thirty-five years were spent married, 61 unmarried. His wife Mary died in 1710 from an injury received from a fall from a horse while she was riding on a pillow behind her husband. They were on their way to Coventry to visit their children. The record reads at Northampton as documented in *Dwight's History of the Strong Family:*

"Oct. 9, 1710, Jedediah Strong, and wife set out early in the morning to visit their children, at Coventry; but when they came against the Fall (at S. Hadley) among the broad smooth stones, the horse's feet slipped up and he fell flat on the off side and by the fall

killed the woman: though she was not quite dead then, but had life in her until the next day - yet never spoke a word."

Jedediah lived in his father's house until old age, then moved to Lebanon, Connecticut. He lived to see the death of his son, Jedediah Jr. who was killed by Indians in 1709.

The Strongs were educated and were aware of the events that were shaping the new land. Following the formation of the Plymouth Colony, the Massachusetts Bay Colony was formed in 1629. By 1640, about 20,000 men, women and children had settled in the colonies. In 1691, the Plymouth and Massachusetts Colonies became a royal colony. Roger Williams, who fell out of favor with the Puritans, founded Rhode Island in 1644. King Charles II decided to take over the Dutch lands in North America. The land was first given to his brother, the Duke of York. The town of New Amsterdam and the colony of New Netherland was renamed New York in 1664.

However, more closely related to the lives of the Strong family were the events in Connecticut. So many settlers moved to Massachusetts Bay Colony during its early years that most of the best land was soon taken. Early Americans then began settling along the fertile valleys of the Connecticut River to the south. By 1635 and 1636, they had built the river towns of Windsor and Wethersfield. In 1636, a clergyman named Thomas Hooker, along with members of his church, founded a third settlement called Hartford. The following year, the three communities united to form the colony of Connecticut. Property owners in the colony who were known as freemen, drew up America's first written plan of government. They called their plan the Fundamental Order of Connecticut. This plan gave freemen the right to elect the colony's governor and all representatives to the lawmaking assembly. It also stated that the government must rest on the will of the people. Like Rhode Island, Connecticut became a self-governing colony. The Strongs were becoming a part of the new American experience.

Jedediah had 14 children. Elizabeth, born in 1664, was the first and Mary was the last, born in 1683. George W. Strong was a descendant of Jedediah Jr., the third child, born in 1667.

Third Generation in America
Jedediah Strong Jr. (1667-1709)

Jedediah Strong Jr. was born on Aug. 7, 1667, in Northampton and lived there as a farmer, marrying Abiah Ingersoll in 1688. She was born in 1663 and was the daughter of John Ingersoll, first of Hartford, then of Northampton, and afterwards of Westfield, Massachusetts. Her mother was Abigail Bascom, the second wife of John Ingersoll. In 1696, Jedediah moved to Lebanon, Connecticut, and was one of only four white families there. No one's name appears more often on the early records of Lebanon as a committee-man on various matters of public interest.

Lebanon became the home of generations of Strongs, some of whom would venture west and settle in the Michigan Territory. Lebanon, Connecticut, was a town with a remarkable history. No town at that time compared with it in the number of leading professional men serving the nation. These great settlers were committed to the worship of God and were of superior stock and the very best intellectuals from Northampton and surrounding towns. The land at Lebanon was the very best quality and rewarding to farmers who were not afraid of hard work.

The children of Jedediah and Abiah were Azariah born 1689, Stephan born 1690, David born 1693, Eleazer born 1695, Supply born 1697, Jedediah born 1700, Ezra born 1701 and Freedom born 1702.

The following letter written by Jedediah Jr. to his son Stephan (then aged 19) , a few months previous to his death is of interest. It is taken from *Dwight's History of the Strong Family*.

"Son Stephan:

"hearty lobe to you, hoping you are well; as I am, blessed be God for it. I have nothing of news to write to you. I wrote a letter to yur mother yesterday, and therein all the news I have: but yet I

15

gladly take the opportunity to write a word to you, as a testification of my love to you. I hope you will be mindful of the advise I left you. Be tender of, and obedient to your mother. I hope you take care of affairs at home; they are but little in my thoughts; but I daily mind you, and God forbid that I should cease to pray for you daily. I want such opportunity for it as I had at home. Dear son, pray for yourself and for me also. Give my respect to your mother. What I here say to you, I herein say to the rest of my dear ones. Also my affectionate love to my dear daughter. Naught else.

I remain your affectionate father,
JEDEDIAH STRONG"

Jedediah was killed by Indians at Wood Creek, New York, October 12, 1709, at the age of 42. For hundreds of years the Indian culture had not changed. Europeans suddenly began to arrive on their lands in the 1600s. The invaders had a very different culture. They had tools and weapons made of iron, a metal the Indians had not learned to make. They also had work animals to help them carry heavy loads and travel long distances. The most important difference was the way the Europeans viewed the land. They believed people had the right to own and work the soil and water on which their lives depended. The Indians believed the land could not be owned in the way people owned weapons, tools or clothing. To the Indian the land was sacred. It was not something to be bought or sold. This difference resulted in bloodshed as the Europeans went about claiming the land. Jedediah Strong Jr. was a victim of this bloodshed. His wife, Abiah, died November 20, 1732, at the age of 69. His son Ezra was 8 years old when his father was killed by Indians. George W. Strong was a descendant of Ezra Strong.

Fourth Generation in America
Ezra Strong (1701 - 1788)

The Michigan Territory was still a wilderness as the villages in the East were growing in both size and stature. Lebanon, Connecticut, was most noted for its grand schools in its early history. In 1700, the town appropriated 200 acres of land for a school and many of the farmers gave parcels of their own land for the school. Notably, Rev. Joseph Parsons gave five acres of his land. In 1740, a grammar school was established by a vote of the town. It became a school of renown having pupils from nine out of the thirteen colonies which composed the Union. The school sent large numbers of its students in successive years to Harvard and Yale.

Here especially, Nathan Tisdale, "Master Tisdale" as he was called, influenced an entire generation. He was a graduate of Harvard and took care of the grammar school for 37 years from his graduation to his death. A number of well-trained minds benefited from his teachings for many years, contributing to the advancement of their day. They included Jeremiah Mason, Zephaniah Swift, Col. John Trumbull, Gov. Jonathan Trumbull Jr., Rev. Dr. Lyman, Judge Baldwin, and a host of others like them. For the Strongs that lived in Lebanon, Connecticut, Master Tisdale was instrumental in their Christian education. Lebanon and similar towns were the foundation for not only Strong descendants but for many of the pioneers who moved West after the War of 1812.

Ezra Strong was the son of Jedediah Jr. born March 2, 1701, and grew up on the farm of his father. He himself became a farmer in Lebanon and married Abigail Caverley in 1730. She was born in 1715 and was the daughter of Philip and Hannah Caverley of Coldhester, Connecticut. Ezra remained in Lebanon, where his first six children were born and he continued to farm.

Farming for Ezra was the same as his father before him and his grandfather before that. The farms were small and the family lived on what they raised, on what were called subsistence farms. The Strong farm had woods, pastures, fields, a vegetable garden and an orchard. The entire family kept busy and each member had a task to perform. Ezra and the older boys cared for the crops and animals. They also chopped wood, built fences and carved wood tools. Abigail and the girls did the cooking and sewing. They had many other tasks. Abigail and the older daughters helped with the harvest, cared for the sick and schooled the young children.

Making linen cloth was a family project. Ezra and the boys began the process by harvesting a plant called flax. They prepared the flax by stripping off or crushing its outer covering. Next Abigail and the girls spun the fiber into linen thread on a spinning wheel. Using a hand loom they wove this thread into cloth. When the cloth was finished, they dyed it with juice of different berries or with bark boiled in water. Less desirable tasks such as making soap or candles were also family tasks. The Strong family and children worked together to try to build a good life in America.

A restless spirit and a growing desire for more land resulted in Ezra's moving to Colchester, Connecticut, for a short while, then to Marlboro, Connecticut, in 1645 where his next six children were born and where he remained until his death. His first son, Ezra, was a farmer and later built a saw mill and a grist mill at Williamsbury, Massachusetts, then a wilderness. He was drafted and went into the Revolutionary Army in 1775. His second son, Jabin, loved to travel and went West without being killed by Indians. Jabin accidentally went over Niagara Falls and survived. Philip was a farmer and a surveyor. Eban was a farmer in Marlboro. Abigail married and lived in Lebanon, Connecticut. Freedom and Lucy married farmers and lived in Marlboro. David was a farmer and a weaver by trade. He was a commissary in the Revolutionary Army. Hannah, Ruby and Lydia all married farmers. The sixth child born to Ezra and Abigail was John Strong. John Strong was the grandfather of George W. Strong.

Fifth Generation in America
John Strong (1743-1791)

America was changing. Ninety percent of new Americans were farmers, but larger cities were emerging. The lure of life near the large towns with its conveniences was beginning to change the face of the colonies. One such town was Glastonbury, Connecticut, and it would draw John Strong to its outskirts. John Strong, the son of Ezra and Abigail Strong, was born December 7, 1743. John was born in Lebanon but spent his early childhood on his father's farm in Marlboro. His memories of Lebanon and Glastonbury 31 miles to its west flamed the young man's dreams.

The Dutch first explored the Connecticut River in 1614. The river was along the western boundaries of the colonies and was the home of the river Indians who belonged to the great confederation known as the Algonquin. The river Indians were great fishermen and made abundant catches of salmon and shad, using nets made of wild hemp. Ducks, wild geese and other waterfowl were plentiful as well as turkeys, partridge, quail and pigeons.

Soon after news of the river spread east, trappers arrived and by 1631 were building forts and trading posts. The settlement of Hartford was founded in 1636. Towns began to spring up near the river as more settlers arrived, including Windsor, Northampton, Lebanon, Wethersfield and Glastonbury. By 1636, Wethersfield consisted of 30 families who had migrated and others were arriving, some directly from England. Settlers then crossed from the west side of the Connecticut River to the east and began what was to become the settlement of Glastonbury. The settlers began a disorganized process of trading with the Indians for land. The King Philip's War (1675-76) marked the final attempt by the Indians to keep the English from taking the land. The demise of the Indian population became inevitable. Deprived of their lands, weakened by rum and subject to diseases passed on to them by the white people, the Indian families along the river gradually died off.

Industry got its start with saw mills because of an abundant supply of water power. Grist mills soon followed. The deep river and an abundant supply of lumber led to shipbuilding and commerce in lumber to the East. The road to Glastonbury was well traveled with taverns along the way. Glastonbury was a resting place for travelers going north and south between Hartford and New Haven as well as

South Glastonbury suburb - Sketch by John Warren, 1836

for those bound east and west using the ferries to cross the river to Gilead, Hebron and Lebanon 31 miles away.

John Strong made the trip from Marlboro to Lebanon, then to Glastonbury in 1763. The area by this time had grown to 4,000 settlers and had developed an industrial base. John was not ready to forgo his roots as a farmer and purchased land just outside the town to do what he knew best, farm. Over the years in Glastonbury, John Strong became a well-known farmer. He married Rachel Curtiss of Colchester, Connecticut, who was born in 1743. The marriage took place in 1765. The couple had four children: John, born 1766; Rachel, born 1768: Gilbert, born 1770 and Betsey, born 1772.

John soon learned that the more populated towns with fledgling industry and frequent communication with the East were also wrought with complexities. Defending the colonies against attack by the French and others had cost the British a great deal of money. As a result, the British had very high taxes in their country. They then decided to shift some of their financial burden to the colonists. The actions of Parliament in 1764 did not excite Glastonbury and John Strong. The following year when Parliament passed the Townshend Act, Glastonbury, like most other towns in the colony, began to resist.

The acts were repealed on all items except tea. The Boston "Sons of Liberty" under Samuel Adams dumped tea into the Boston Harbor one night which led to the Revolution. Three weeks later, June 23, 1774, a town meeting was called at which the citizens supported Boston and the patriots in resisting the tyranny of the British.

The Stamp Act of 1765, which taxed all legal documents, newspapers and other documents, was met with a great uproar in the Colonies. In 1766, this tax was repealed, but it was just the beginning of the problems between the colonists and the British. The Boston Tea Party in 1773 was an act of revolt against the British and their tax on tea in the Colonies.

Tensions such as these eventually led to the writing of the Declaration of Independence in 1776. A year earlier, the War of Independence, also known as the American Revolution, began. The British soldiers fired on the line of farmer-patriots at Lexington on April 19, 1775 and news of the event reached Glastonbury the following day. Two days later the drums beat and the call to arms went out: *War has begun. Our men have been fired upon at Lexington and at Concord. Send help at once*. At daybreak of the following day, 59 men led by Captain Elizur Hubbard began the march to Boston. Among the 59 men was George Stocking, the future father-in-law of John Strong Jr. The men returned a short time later with news that the British had retreated. In the weeks and months that followed, the War for Independence intensified and many from Glastonbury and the Colonies gave their lives for liberty. John Strong and his generation experienced the American Revolution. The news and events that were taking place were a dominant part of everyday life. John and family members conversed frequently on the unfolding events, but John, with children ages 4 to 10, did not answer the call to arms.

Among those of the Strongs who fought as officers in the War were Lieutenant-Colonel David and Chaplains Joseph and Nathan of Connecticut, Captain Nathan of New York, and Captain Solomon of Connecticut. Many of the Strongs were citizens of the colonies who fought and died during the Revolutionary War.

Perhaps the most famous was Nathan Hale. Nathan was the son of Elizabeth Strong, a fifth generation descendant through Thomas Strong, and Richard Hale. Nathan Hale was an extremely bright lad who attended Yale in 1769, where he distinguished himself as a scholar, especially in languages and fine literature. After college, he taught school with great zest in Connecticut. When the news of the battle of Lexington reached New London, he was among the first to defy the British aggression in public saying "Let us march immediately and never lay down our arms until we obtained our independence."

He enrolled at once as a volunteer and temporarily closed his school. On July 6, 1775, he enlisted as a lieutenant in the third company of the seventh Connecticut regiments where he was shortly made Captain. In April 1776, he went with troops under General Keyes to New York where the Battle of Long Island was taking place. General Washington felt that someone must penetrate the British camp on the Island and learn the sequence of their movements. Nathan volunteered for the mission. He posed as a Dutch artist speaking Dutch fluently and sent information and sketches back to the Colonial army. Nathan Hale was discovered and captured by the British and sentenced to be hanged on September 22, 1776. His last words were: "*I regret that I have but one life to give for my country*." The British officers were so impressed by the courage of the 21-year-old young man that they informed the Colonial Army of his last words.

Grandparents of George Strong - The Stockings

Glastonbury was an important supplier to the Revolutionary War effort. Its largest industry at this period was a gunpowder factory located on the north bank of Roaring Brook in South Glastonbury, at Cotton Hollow run by George Stocking Sr., and his sons. The Stocking mill was one of the few powder plants in New England which helped to supply ammunition for General Washington's army. That it managed to do so was a tribute to the courage of one of the unsung heroines of the Revolutionary War, Eunice Cobb Stocking. On August 23, 1777, a fire broke out in the Stocking factory and touched off an explosion which destroyed the mill and killed six men. Mrs. Stocking had driven a load of gunpowder to the outskirts of Boston and was returning when, going through Bolton Notch, 15 miles from home, she felt the ground tremble and saw a cloud of black smoke to the west. Horrified, for there was no mistaking what had happened, she urged her horse on homewards as fast as he could make it. Her loss was great. Killed in the explosion were her husband and three of her sons, George, Jr., Hezakiah and Nathaniel. The only remaining son, Elisha, had been sent on an errand and escaped the explosion. Mrs. Stocking was endowed with great courage. She enlisted the financial help of Howell Woodbridge, rebuilt the factory and continued to supply gunpowder for the Army until the end of the war. The Daughters of the American Revolution have honored the memory of Eunice Cobb Stocking by giving her name to the Glastonbury Chapter. When the war was over, Mrs. Stocking took on the operation of the former Bidwell grist mill across the brook from the powder mill, which her husband had bought before his tragic death.

When the British finally surrendered on October 19, 1781, Americans were officially independent of Britain and set about establishing their own government.

John Strong Sr. was a farmer, as his father and grandfather before him. John aided the war effort by providing supplies from the farm. John died in 1791, and was survived by Rachel who moved to Pawley, Vermont after his death, where she married for a second time. His daughter, Rachel, remained in Glastonbury and another daughter, Betsey, moved to Pawley where she died. Gilbert became a successful farmer on the "German Flats". John Strong Jr., the father of George W. Strong, was to become a part of the changing America.

| 1798 | | 1812-15 | | 1825 |
| Alien and Sedition Acts | | War of 1812 | | Erie Canal completed |

	1803		1820		1836
	Lousiana Purchase		Missouri		Trail of Tears
			Compromise		

1776		1804-08		1823		1852
Independence		Lewis & Clark		Monroe		National
Day		expedition		Doctrine		Road
						completed

American History

Chapter 2 - Manifest Destiny and George W. Strong

Sixth Generation in America
John Strong Jr. (1766 - 1840)

John Strong Jr. was born April 26, 1766. He would experience life in what was a large urban village at the time. Villages grew within traveling distance of most farms. Many farmers lived in Glastonbury and went out each day to work in the fields. Farmers no longer had to make or raise everything they needed. They could go to Glastonbury or Westerfield to buy or trade goods. There they would find a grist mill for grinding grain and a blacksmith shop for shoeing their horses or mules. They could also shop in stores which sold goods made in Europe. Trade developed along the Connecticut River, bringing goods from the East. There were warehouses, ships and shipbuilding which made Glastonbury, with a population of 4,000, different from most towns. This was a large city considering the population of the colonies was 2.7 million of which 20% were slaves.

In the spring of 1777, all Glastonbury buzzed with excitement when a group of Yale students arrived to hold classes there. For some months, the Yale administration, facing wartime shortages, had problems trying to provide adequate food for the students. In late March, President Naphtili Daggett decided to disperse the student body to several inland towns until provisions were more plentiful. There was also some concern that New Haven might be invaded by the British. Glastonbury was one of several towns which issued an invitation to the university. Probably the invitation came from William Wells, who had been a Yale tutor. William's son, William, Jr. was a member of the sophomore class at the time. Under the supervision of Professor Nehemiah Strong (a Strong family descendant) and the Rev. Joseph Buckminster, a tutor, the Yale sophomores and juniors were sent to Glastonbury. Seniors went to Westerfield and freshmen to Farmington. Classes began about April in the home of William Wells and ended about June of the following year. Two of the children who attended the classes were John Strong Jr. and Sabra

Stocking. Among the students was Noah Webster, whose dictionary and blue-blacked speller later became bestsellers.

The summer of 1777 was a reminder that the Revolutionary War was not only being fought in the East but was a part of life in Glastonbury. The gunpowder factory disaster was well remembered by young John Strong, and he knew that it was the family of Sabra Stocking which suffered the death of Mr. Stocking and his sons.

Events such as the second Continental Congress and the Declaration of Independence did not mean much to the 10 year old John Strong Jr., but all adults were talking about nothing else. As he grew older, he became more aware of unfolding events. The Battle of Bunker Hill, the emergence of General George Washington, the crossing of the Delaware River, Saratoga the turning point, and finally the British surrender at Yorktown in 1781 became meaningful events.

The war years were difficult for everyone in Glastonbury. Trade had come to a halt and the efforts of everyone were directed to supporting the war. At one point in time, food was so scarce that the farmers cut cornstalks and crushed them in cider mills, and then boiled the juice down to syrup as a substitute for sugar. During the course of the war, taxes went up steadily, reaching two shillings and a sixpence on one pound's assessment, the equivalent of an assessment of 125 mills. The soldiers' wages paid by the State were small, and the town at various times voted extra pay as an inducement for enlistment. The measure was successful, for at various times nearly every able-bodied man of fighting age was in the service. The children and women did much of the work in the fields during this time and Mrs. Eunice Cobb Stocking, grandmother to George W. Strong, rebuilt and ran the gunpowder factory, becoming one of the most recognized American women by the Daughters of the American Revolution.

Another change was taking place among the young people of Glastonbury. They were exposed to some diverse ideas as learning stimulated their minds. Students formed a drama group and rehearsed the play, *Tancred and Sigismunda*, hoping to put on a performance for a local audience. The sober-minded Glastonbury villagers, still under the domination of the Puritan church, would have none of it. Anything having to do with liberal teachers was considered immoral. Not to be cheated of their efforts, the group hired the State House in Hartford and performed there. This was one of the first forms of democratic protest by young people. John Strong and Sabra Stocking, who were growing into adulthood, would take sides in this debate. Sabra, urbanized and a member of a wealthy family, was more liberal than John who had deep roots in both farming and a Puritan background. Their differences did not deter their attraction for each other.

Changes were taking place in the colonies as John entered adulthood. The Articles of Confederation were adopted the same year the Revolutionary War ended. A land ordinance was passed in 1785 and a Constitutional Convention was convened in 1786. These events were not foremost on the mind of John Strong Jr. A growing interest was developing between John Strong and Sabra Stocking despite their opposite lifestyle.

Comfortable Glastonbury home in 1755

The advice from parents supported the lifestyles to which each was accustomed. Their young love resulted in marriage on September 25, 1786, when both were 20 years old.

There are always compromises in marriages. This was especially true for Sabra. She had enjoyed the comfortable living of urban life as a result of her parents' owning the largest business in Glastonbury. It is said that opposites attract, which was surely the case for the young married couple. Sabra was like most women of the time as she adopted the lifestyle of her husband and was introduced to the life of a farmer. After the war, life reverted back to normal as trade and agriculture both prospered. The country was celebrating a new constitution in 1788, and John and Sabra were parents for the first time with the birth of a son, John Strong III, born April 13, 1788. The names of Thomas Jefferson and Alexander Hamilton were household words, as were their new ideas. George Washington was the first President of the United States when a daughter, Sabra, was born on May 22, 1790. Hamilton set up a new banking system in 1791 and the Strongs were involved in the confusing exercise of converting the different types of European currencies to American dollars. The following year, their third child, Ira, was born February 15, 1792, followed by Sheldon, born June 16, 1794, and Lucy, born June 12, 1796.

Another first was to take place in 1793. Two political parties were emerging in America. Alexander Hamilton and Thomas Jefferson became bitter political enemies. By the end of 1793, the differences between the two men were too great to settle. Jefferson resigned from Washington's cabinet and returned to Virginia. He then began to organize his followers into a political party. Because of Jefferson's action, Hamilton was forced to resign from the Cabinet in 1795. Hamilton in turn organized his followers into a party to oppose Jefferson's group. Jefferson's party was known as the Democratic-Republican Party. This marked the beginning of the Strong family's commitment to a political party. John Strong considered himself a Jeffersonian Democrat. This was in conflict with the preferences of his mother-in-law, Eunice Stocking, who preferred the views of Hamilton.

Most of the farmers like Jefferson opposed the idea of a strong national government. They also were opposed to the leadership of the educated wealthy. Hamilton worked with John Adams of Massachusetts to found a second political party. Adams had been a member of the committee which wrote the Declaration of Independence. He was also George Washington's Vice President. The followers of Adams and Hamilton believed in a strong national government with broad powers. They looked to the wealthy, successful, educated citizens for leadership. Hamilton's party was called the Federalist Party.

By 1796, differences were taking place not only in the evolving government of America but also between John and Sabra. Sabra had always been close to her mother, especially after the loss of her father and two brothers in the factory disaster. The successful Eunice Stocking was a Federalist. On the other hand, John was a farmer and a strong supporter of Jefferson. John cast his vote for Jefferson in 1796, but Adams was elected the second President of the United States. John and Sabra had been living in Glastonbury for 32 years when Polly was born on December 22, 1798. John was reaching a turning point in his life. His Strong roots were beginning to stir the restless spirit in him and the desire for more land and a larger farm became an obsession. Sabra was expecting her seventh child in 1799. This child would be the first child born in the new century. Both she and her mother felt differently about this child. Sabra had grown closer to her mother drawn by the fear that the new century would find her leaving Glastonbury.

Seventh Generation in America
George Stocking Strong

The seventh child of John and Sabra was born on February 15, 1800. John agreed to have his son's middle name christened Stocking at the request of Sabra. A special bond developed between the young George and his mother. One more son was born in Glastonbury and it would be the last Strong child born in Connecticut for the couple. Ansel Strong was born February 15, 1802.

The Strong descendants had increased in numbers in the East

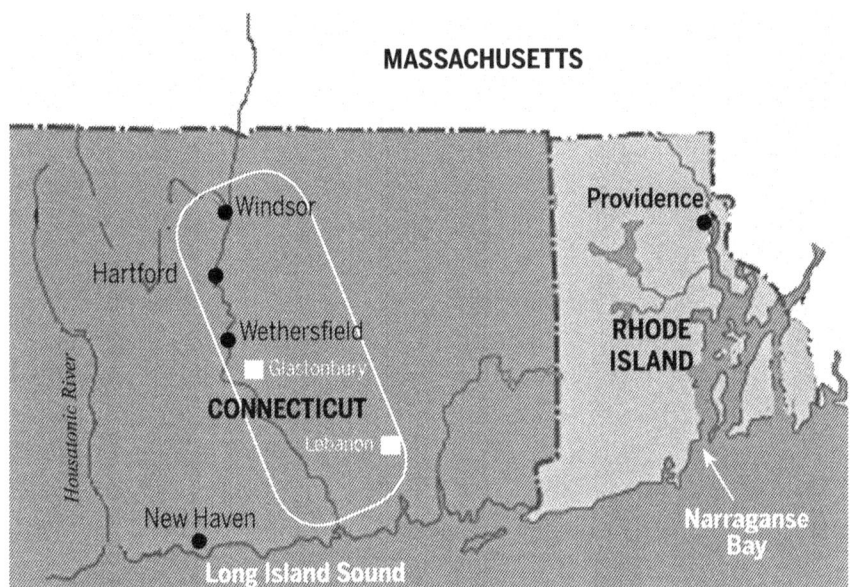

Home to six generations of Strongs

by 1800. The men worked hard and lived long lives. It was not uncommon for their wives to have twelve to fourteen children.

The hard life of the mothers and the number of children they had to bear resulted in the husbands outliving the wives. If the offspring survived childhood diseases and the Indian attacks, they continued the practice of having large families. A Strong could have twenty uncles and aunts and seventy cousins. Most were literate and kept in communication with each other by mail. John occasionally received letters from his mother who had remarried in Pawley, Vermont.

Pawley was a few short miles from Montpelier. Letters always included the lure of good land and few people. Success for John was with the land. For generations, the desire for land was the motivating force in the movement to America. Self-gratification was directly related to a flourishing large farm. He could not relate to the idea that an industrialized America would one day change that dream. He could not accept as true that the lifestyle in Glastonbury was the America of the future. The dream of larger farms, together with his restless spirit, shaped the future of John Strong from 1803 to his death. Influenced by his mother and the old ways, John, at the age of 37, decided to leave Glastonbury in 1803 and travel north along the Connecticut River. It was a culture shock for Sabra as the family traveled north to Pawley, Vermont, through the wilderness. It was a most difficult time for Sabra. She agreed to leave her home of thirty five years. She knew that she would never return and could not look back. Traveling 200 miles by ox and horse along a turbulent river to the unknown was overwhelming. Sabra knew that it was her duty to follow her husband as the family of eight, the oldest 15, and the youngest 1, followed the Connecticut River to Paunorth. All possessions were left behind, taking only what pioneers needed to survive, using horses and a wagon drawn by oxen. The trails along the river were well-traveled first by the Indians and later by settlers. There were small settlements and farms along the way. The family arrived at Bath, New Hampshire, 200 miles from their old home, after a summer of travel in 1803.

Bath was a place to rest after the long journey. A new grist mill had just been built and the settlement consisted of about 20 families. Bath, New Hampshire, had one of the few crossing points on the Connecticut River to Vermont. John became familiar with the area and was attracted to the settlement of Ryegate twelve miles to the west in Vermont with a population of 300 settlers. The family crossed the Connecticut River and followed the Wells River to Ryegate in 1805 and built a log home on a small farm. While they were in Ryegate, four more children were born. Eunice was born in 1806, William in 1807, Francis in 1808 and Elvira in 1812. Sabra was ailing when John moved again to Newbury, Vermont, with Sabra and the younger children in 1814. Newbury would be the final resting place for Sabra as she passed away later that year. The pioneer life had taken its toll on Sabra, leaving behind twelve children. She never again saw the urban life she remembered and loved.

War of 1812

Events were taking place in America that would later influence the choices of first George and Ansel Strong and later Ira and Eunice, who would venture to Michigan. The Strong family could relate to the importance of shipping because they were never far from a river. The Connecticut River was one of the main shipping routes to the ocean and flowed for over 250 miles.

The British had a love/hate relationship with the Colonies. They had been inciting the Indians, interfering with shipping and kidnapping sailors to help fight the war with Napoleon. President Madison asked Congress to declare the war of 1812 and Congress approved over the Federalists' objections. The British were skilled soldiers in contrast to the Americans who were young, inexperienced and with no navy. The first battles were against the British in Canada to the north and west. They proved to be bitter defeats and embarrassments with the fall of Detroit and Frenchtown in the Michigan territory. The Americans countered with an attack on York in Canada, burning the British capital. This incited the British, and after defeating Napoleon, they brought the force of their power to America. The British were able to march against Washington in April of 1814 and set the Capitol on fire. Following this bitter defeat for the Americans, the British forces then moved against Baltimore. This time, Baltimore was ready. A 30 by 40 foot flag was ordered for Fort McHenry as it prepared to defend the harbor. The assault by the British began on September 13, 1814. During the assault on Fort McHenry, British shells and rockets turned the skies of Baltimore fiery red. Francis Scott Key remained on deck of a British ship watching throughout the night. The firing continued all day into the next night. When dawn came, the sound of bursting shells had ceased. Key saw the American flag still flying. Deeply moved, Key composed a poem describing the events he witnessed. The words became known as the "Star-Spangled Banner." The British fleet left Baltimore and turned their attention to New Orleans. The war ended when General Andrew Jackson defeated the British in the battle of New Orleans. A new spirit of greatness came over America. It began a new age and Manifest Destiny began a great movement west.

Sabra was the force that had held the family together. Her death came as the War of 1812 was ending. Her daughters were at her side in her final years, but shortly after her passing they would go their separate ways. Lucy was married in 1815 to William Scott of Newbury. John was next to marry in 1816 to Nancy McNaught of Pawley, and he became a cotton and woolen mill manufacturer.

Daughter Sabra married Robert Brooks in 1816. George and Ansel who were close in age became very close as brothers. They were both among their mother's favorites and the last children born in Glastonbury.

Sabra's Influence on Young George

Sabra thought that George would be the last of her children born in Glastonbury due to her husband's desire for land. She thought by giving him the middle name Stocking it would be a reminder of the home and family she would one day leave. One more son, Ansel, was born just as final plans were made to leave the town. Sabra made a special effort to share memories of life in Glastonbury with the younger children. She could see George and Ansel had very different interests. George was creative and venturesome. As he played along the rivers, Sabra could see he was fearless. The land and farming did not hold his attention. Most pleasing, he had a genuine interest in tales of urban life which he had never experienced. George marveled as Sabra told him of the success of Grandfather Stocking and Sabra's early days. When grandfather died in the explosion, grandmother was able to put the tragedy behind her and start over again. Life will have its ups and downs but the bad times did not stop the Stockings. She kept reminding George that he could one day also reach great heights and do anything he set his mind to. He might even one day help build a city like Glastonbury. Ansel, on the other hand, took his mother's past more lightly and was his father's son. He would one day follow the traditional family desire to farm.

George and Ansel were home-schooled as youngsters by both the older sisters and Sabra. When one room schoolhouses were available in Rygate and Newbury, the boys attended. Both boys worked on the farm as their father directed. George objected, but worked because of a sense of duty. He worked on a farm for the last time at the age of 17. Seizing an early opportunity, he went into a partnership with his older brother, John, and ran a woolen mill in Chelsea, Vermont. George saw that his future would be in business, realizing that his mother may have been correct in her advice. His break with the past took another turn when he changed his name to suit his new future profession, although he did not know what it would be. George Stocking Strong became George Washington Strong, hence **George W. Strong**.

George developed a friendship with Hannah Vickers who was a year younger and the daughter of a farmer living in Chelsea. Although he was successful in business, George planned to save enough money to study medicine. He developed a friendship with a local doctor who tutored and counseled him in medicine. It did not take long for George to tire of both the woolen mill and medicine. Not sure of where the future would take him, George tried a little of everything, including shipping, building and even playing the loom as a musician. George remained friends with Hannah Vickers and the two were married September 20, 1822. They made their home in Stockbridge, Vermont, where their first two children were born, George Albert on July 20, 1824, and Helen on June 18, 1825.

The West, which was the Michigan Territory, began to open up after the War of 1812. Indians were not as much a threat, and there were few people and vast expanses of good farmland. Ansel looked up to his older brother although their dreams were different. The brothers began thinking both their dreams might be fulfilled in the West. The planning began for one last bold move into a new unknown, one to farm and the other to help build a city.

George W. Strong, who had traveled from one small settlement to another, and Hannah, who knew only life on a farm, made the decision to go west in 1824. The citizens of Vermont knew well the account of the capture of Fort Ticonderoga by Ethan Allan and the 83 Green Mountain Boys. Ticonderoga was an ideal location to cross Lake Champlain and proceed to the ultimate destination of the St. Lawrence River. In time, George could follow the River to the Great Lakes and Michigan.

The journey began in the summer of 1826 for Ansel, George, Hannah and the two children. Horses, a wagon, an ox and the few possessions they could carry, along with the two infants, were all they needed to make the journey. Their first destination was the St. Lawrence Seaway and Fort Ticonderoga which was 77 miles away. The first part of the journey was safe with settlements and farms along the way. They crossed Lake Champlain on barges at Ticonderoga and purchased supplies for the next leg of the journey. The next 150 miles through New York to the St. Lawrence were more hazardous and sparsely populated. The Strongs followed a series of Indian trails along the rivers until they came upon the Raquette River. There, they found the settlement of Norfolk located ten miles from the St. Lawrence River. George W. Strong arrived in Norfolk, New York, late in the year 1826 and decided to make this their home for a short time.

Norfolk, New York

Norfolk was founded by the families of Hale and Bradley who settled in the southwest part of the town in 1823. Bernard Smith from Ireland settled in the northwest of the town a few years later. Other families settled around Raymondville nearby. The area was mostly a wilderness located along the Racquette River between Potsdam and Massera. The town had a population of 200 people when the Strongs arrived. The area saw quick growth and became a major blue collar community of saw mills, paper mills, grist mills and woolen factories.

George and Ansel proceeded to build a structure of logs which would be George's new home. The most important item in outfitting the home was a great iron pot and a copper kettle. The iron pot hung in the fireplace and could hold as much as ten gallons of water. All types of vegetables were boiled by Hannah to become a main part of the meal and a Dutch oven was used to cook the meat and baked goods. There was no control of natural light or darkness. Light had to come from nature. Different types of candles were extinguished early in order to save every penny and the fireplace provided light at bedtime. Hannah made soap, which was a task she dreaded, but was the only means for bodily cleanliness. The skills of basket weaving and making maple sugar were learned from the Indians. Many of the cures for sickness also came from the Indians. George Albert and Helen were home-schooled by neighbors until the area built its first one-room schoolhouse. The only mode of transportation was the horse and wagon. There was no local newspaper, but letters and papers from the East arrived by mail. Information from 41 travelers was also valuable. The next four Strong children were born in Norfolk, New York: Thomas in 1827 and the twins, Thurlow and Alonzo in 1830, followed by William in 1835.

Shortly after arriving in Norfolk, a change of plans was necessary. Hannah was pregnant again with another child and the stay in Norfolk was extended for George Strong. Ansel, on the other hand, elected to proceed to Michigan. Although George Strong was successful in the growing town of Norfolk, he saw that it was like every other town that he lived in except Glastonbury. He did not remember Glastonbury, but saw it through the eyes of his mother.

Ansel returned from the Michigan Territory, where he had acquired land in Jackson, Michigan, in 1828 and left a new bride behind. Ansel also had news of the Erie Canal, which was nearing completion near Buffalo and the settlement of Frenchtown, which was growing rapidly and land was at a premium. Jackson, forty miles away, had better farmland at a bargain. The county had only 3,000 settlers, most living in Frenchtown and it was growing unlike anything ever seen in Vermont. Ansel returned to Jackson, Michigan, in 1831 and never ventured east again.

Manifest Destiny began in 1832 for George W. Strong when he traveled to Michigan for the first time after the birth of twins in 1830. His family would join him in 1835. George had no idea what awaited him across two Great Lakes at the gateway to the west, **Frenchtown.** Brother Ira married Fanny Harsome in 1825 and moved to Glenn Falls, New York. Later Ira also moved to Michigan and became successful in the lumber business. Brother Shelden married Martha Stratton of Chelsea in 1830. He became a successful cotton manufacturer in Chelsea. Their father, John Strong, died in 1840 in Stockbridge, Vermont, and left little to his children.

Chapter 3 - The Lure of Frenchtown

To the north of the Colonies was a vast land, Canada that was being explored by the French. A French sailor-soldier named Champlain traveled up the St. Lawrence River with a group of settlers in 1608. When he spotted a high cliff overlooking the river, Champlain picked it for a settlement. He thought the location would be easy to defend. The first French settlement was named Quebec. Champlain continued to explore the river and discovered Montreal in 1614 and Lakes Huron and Ontario. La Salle followed in 1679-82, exploring Lake Erie, the Detroit River, Lake Michigan and then on to the Mississippi River.

For a century and a half following the discovery of the Great Lakes, commerce was chiefly furs. It was a valuable trade. The lakes were surrounded by nearly a thousand miles of shoreline, and by means of portages gave ready access to a still wider scope of country inland, inhabited only by roving bands of savages and wild animals. When the Canadian settlements were established, trade quickly sprang up with the natives, and the Indians made voyages from the upper lake region to Montreal to exchange furs and pelts for the weapons and cheap ornaments of the immigrants. For a long series of years, Montreal was the center of a large and profitable trade. Thousands of Frenchmen from all grades of life came over to better their fortunes, and ships bearing the white banners of France crossed the Atlantic, carrying westward passengers and supplies and returning with a freight of furs.

Fur Traders and Farmers

The earliest demand for furs was supplied by the Indians. As the helpless beaver, mink and otter became exterminated; the hardy *voyageurs* pushed and rowed their *bateaux* in all directions, yet made their home in Montreal, where they spent the winters in rioting on the savings of the summers. Still later, it was necessary to establish frontier stations to serve as outposts for the merchants of Montreal, and this movement stimulated exploration. The trading post and the mission house were the two types of French occupation on the shores of the lakes.

The French pioneers discovered that as the Indians were ignorant of the value of the furs they accumulated, enormous profit was possible for the successful trader in furs. In the infancy of this industry, there was absolutely no limit to the percentage of profit, as the Indians would exchange the most valuable pelts for European trinkets that were worth nothing except the cost of transportation.

The fur trade of Canada produced a class of men who were hardy, agile and fearless with habits approximating the savage. The fur traders were a peculiar class of men, known by the appropriate name of Bush Rangers, half-civilized vagrants, who traveled by canoe along the lakes and rivers of the interior. Many of them, shaking loose every tie of blood and kindred, identified themselves with the Indians and sank into utter barbarism. George W. Strong had known English colonists who were trappers and traders along the St. Lawrence River while in Norfolk, New York. They did not mingle with the Indians and did not believe in race mixing. The English fur-traders, and the rude men in their employ, were not what George would call civilized but did not bear the habits of the Indians.

Not only did the Indians show the French how to find and trap the muskrat and beaver but also how to cook and eat them. This was another experience that the English and George Strong did not relish or pursue.

The character of many of the French trappers gave offense to the missionaries in their efforts to convert the Indians to Catholicism. Complaints were made, and the Canadian government finally decreed that no one should trade with the Indians unless provided with a license.

Not all French were fur traders. Some fished for a living. A few set up small businesses. Others built farms in Nova Scotia and through much of the St. Lawrence valley. The life of most French farmers in America was like that of French peasants in Europe. In France, nobles owned large estates and peasants planted and harvested the crops. The French king set up a similar system in America. To encourage people to settle in New France, the king gave nobles large

On to Detroit

grants of land. The farmers who worked the land continued to give the nobles a part of their crops, much as they had done in France. The farmers did not like the system but could not change it and had no voice in the government.

On to Detroit

On June 5, 1701, Antoine Cadillac, then 43, left a settlement near Montreal and began a journey that would result in the settlement of Detroit. He was in command of 25 long canoes, 100 Frenchmen and about 100 Indians. The party rowed 12 miles west to the mouth of the Ottawa River and then rowed 180 miles upstream reaching Lake Nipissing. The party then rowed across the lake and out the French River nearly 100 miles to reach the Georgian Bay. Cadillac followed the eastern shore of Lake Huron to Port Huron, some 250 miles from the French River. The swift current of the St. Clair River quickly carried them 30 miles to Lake St. Clair. By July 24, 1701, he had reached the area which became known as Detroit.

A fort was established and French trappers and farmers soon began arriving. Ribbon farms, narrow land starting at the River and one to two miles deep, were claimed by the French.

By 1751, the fort survived attacks by Indians and had grown to 483 people, 471 cows, and 160 horses. Unlike the New Englanders

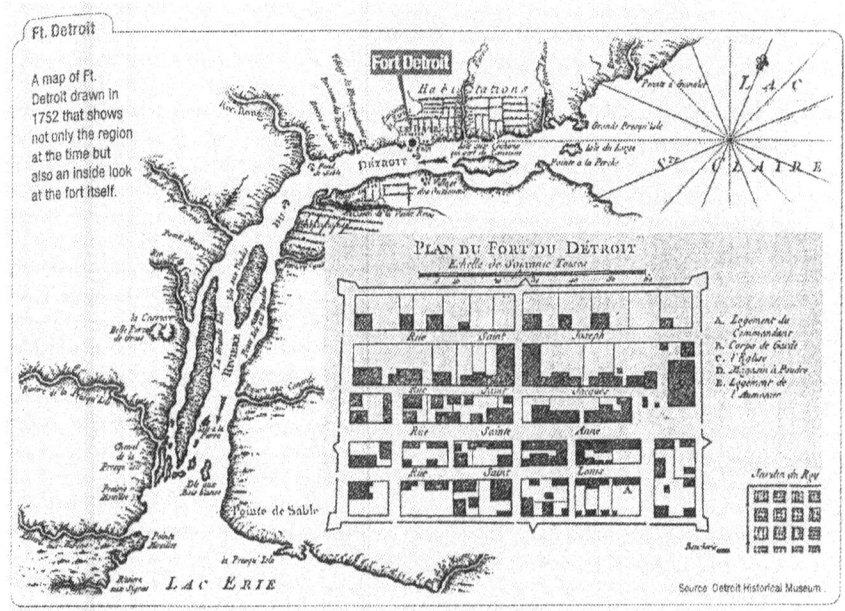

Early map of Detroit

and George Strong, once the French found larger parcels of woods and fertile farmland they were less likely to move.

French and Indian War and the Americans

The Colonists under George Washington tried to stop the French expansion in the Ohio Valley but to no avail. In 1754, the Colonists sought help from the English who immediately sent troops and over a period of seven years, with the help of the Colonists, defeated the French and Indians.

Events took an unfortunate turn for the French in 1760. Fort Detroit was among the spoils of the French and Indian War and Detroit became the property of the English. French settlers adjusted to English occupation but the Indians were wary. The English were not as generous in paying for pelts and were more territorial. The Ottawa Chief, Pontiac, attacked the English who had taken possession of Detroit in 1763. Pontiac was defeated after a short war and the transformation of Detroit from French to English began. What began with the soldiers was completed by settlers from the East.

French Pride

Europe was the homeland for many of the pioneers. Europe was hundreds of centuries old and although it carried on the tradition of western culture, it did not develop a form of government that gave its masses the freedom required to prosper. The American and French Revolutions began a change that is still taking place today. It was the age of enlightenment in Europe. At the same time that the French settlers were moving beyond Detroit, the French Revolution was taking place in Europe beginning on July 14, 1789. A Parisian mob stormed the city jail, The Bastille, released the prisoners, killed the guards and warden, and then paraded around Paris with the heads of the slain people on a pole. Within three years, France was proclaimed a republic. France was rallying against German invaders intent on returning their ruler cousin, Louis XVI, to the throne. For the next three years, France endured a reign of terror trying to determine what to do with the King. That was settled when Louis XVI tried to flee Paris and was captured. He was tried by a tribunal, sentenced and beheaded. His Austrian Princess wife, Queen Marie Antoinette succumbed to the same fate a few months later. Around 1893, a young field artillery lieutenant, Napoleon Bonaparte, began his rise to power. It is hard to imagine today the sheer amount of change that was impacted by the French Revolution. The French Revolution occurred in what was the most advanced country of the day. France was also the most powerful country in Europe and was the center of the Enlightenment and intellectual movement. The French led the world in science. French was the internationally spoken language of intellectuals and aristocrats and French books were read everywhere. The French had the largest and wealthiest European population under a single government with 25 million people. French trade was larger than that of Great Britain. Most gold pieces in circulation in Europe were French. Europeans of the 18th century were in the habit of taking ideas from France and were horrified when the Revolution broke out in that country. This was the first huge political European movement of the Enlightenment. Revolution and change became the new order and a victory for the common person.

That spirit of nationalism and pride remained with the French settlers as they traveled from Quebec to Montreal, then on to Detroit and finally to Frenchtown. The spirit of nationalism was so ingrained in the French Canadians that they were reluctant early on to accept the language and customs of the English speaking Americans. The same strong conviction was also seen in their Catholic faith. The Catholic Church was the only church in Michigan until settlers from the east began coming to the Michigan Territory after the French and Indian War. They were reformed Christians and Protestants. The territory was about to begin a religious transformation.

1780 Navarre to the River Raisin

The Navarres were one of the early white families to settle in Detroit. Francis Navarre, like many of the French, was not comfortable with the changes taking place in Detroit. Francis Navarre ventured 35 miles south in search of a new home site. He was the first to follow the Indian trail south along the lakes on the road that is now Old Dixie to the next large river, the Namet Cybi as the Pottawatamie called it. Later, it was named the River Raisin. Navarre was one of the first known pioneers to settle near the banks of the River Raisin where the Winchester Street bridge is now located. Frenchtown began like most early American settlements. Just as in Glastonbury, Stockbridge, Chelsea and Norfolk where George Strong traveled, a

Early Frenchtown home.

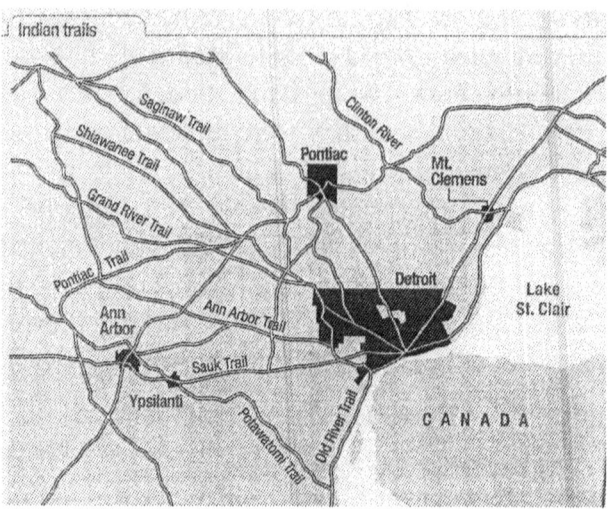

To River Raisin

settlement began with the venturesome spirit of a pioneer. Francis Navarre found a peaceful river surrounded by good farm land, plenty of virgin timber, wild game of all types and of course, Indians. The first pioneer settlers were his family and close friends of his kind, and a village was born. The pioneers saw that the land had an abundance of game. Ducks, bald eagles, muskrats, beaver, red fox, and wild turkey could be found in the forests. Every type of common bird could be seen and heard. The soil was easy to clear and the seasons were good for growing. Beneath the soil was an abundant supply of limestone. The river and creeks provided an unlimited supply of fresh water. Ownership of the land was transferred from the Indians to the settlers soon after their arrival and by 1784 there were one hundred French families, and the foundation of Frenchtown village was laid. The slowly growing French settlement was later recognized as an American settlement and the American flag was raised by Captain Procter in 1796.

Religion in the Early Settlement

France had its share of turmoil in Europe but, unlike Great Britian, remained Catholic. It was the France of Joan of Arc, the patron saint. The French coming to the new land brought their religion with them. They also brought the Black Robes who were intent on spreading

French settlers and Indians

their religion to the Indians. The importance of religion and God can be seen in Frenchtown with the first community building being a church.

In 1788, there were 39 settlers representing most families in Frenchtown who petitioned the Diocese of Detroit to establish a Catholic church on the banks of the River Raisin. Names such as Dubriel, Ledux, Bordeau, Labaux, Godfroy, and Cousino were among the petitioners. The Church of St. Anthony was the name given to the first church in Frenchtown, located two and one-half miles west from where the current St. Mary's Church was built in 1839. The site along the north side of the River Raisin was chosen as the most central in the River Raisin settlement and most convenient to be reached by the inhabitants. It would be thirty-three years after St. Anthony's was built that there would be enough settlers south of the river in Erie Township for the second Roman Catholic Church to be built in 1819.

The arrival of the Americans to Frenchtown also meant the arrival of the Protestant religions to the area. Puritan congregations had given way to the denominational Methodist, Presbyterian and Episcopalian religions. The first Protestant preachers came to Monroe between 1806 and 1810. Rev. William Mitchell, a minister with the Methodist Church, organized a Methodist Episcopal Church, consisting of some two dozen members, in 1811. The two dozen members represented most of the population on the south side of the river. Their efforts were short-lived as the War of 1812 broke out and many of the American families fled the area and moved to Ohio. The work of the church was not taken up again until 1817 when Joseph Mitchell re-established the Methodist church and the Americans began returning to Frenchtown. The services were held in the homes of the members and were very irregular. The Methodists decided to build a church on Monroe Street in 1836 for its growing membership. Rev. John Montecito became the first resident Presbyterian pastor in 1816. He organized the First Presbyterian Church in Monroe in 1820. This was also the first of the English-speaking, Christian churches to be founded in Monroe. The first services were held in a brick home on the corner of Front and Washington Streets. The denomination welcomed other English-speaking Christians such as Congregationalists, Methodists, Baptists, and Episcopalians. The congregation continued to grow to over 100 members and in 1833, a difference among members caused a split to take place; then in 1837, a second Presbyterian Church was formed. The Protestant denominations continued to grow in numbers and it would take years for the community to be comfortable with both the Catholic and Protestant religions.

War of 1812

The Territory of Michigan was organized in 1805 and General Hull was appointed Governor. In the following years, the government of the territory was being formed, with Frenchtown, the second oldest settlement next to Detroit, playing an important role. Few new settlers including militia from the east had joined the community by 1812. Events then unfolded that would affect the settlement of Frenchtown and would change its makeup forever. The surrender of Detroit to the British by General Hull on the 16th of August 1812 at the beginning of the War of 1812 was a bitter setback for the new nation and for President Madison. As a result, the settlement of Frenchtown was occupied by the British and Indians who pillaged and harassed the settlers. Skirmishes resulted in the death of a number of the settlers. American military, Kentucky soldiers and French settlers under the command of General Winchester drove out the British and Indians in January 1813. Three days later, the British regrouped and mounted a counterattack, capturing General Winchester and defeating the American Army in Frenchtown. The battle was a massacre with the British recapturing Frenchtown. Settlers fled seeking safety from the Indians who were looting and killing all but a few remaining settlers. The French fled to safety near Detroit and the Americans to Ohio leaving Frenchtown almost deserted. The British went as far as to suggest that the Indians take back the land from the French settlers. The battle became known as the Frenchtown Massacre and "Remember the Raisin" became a battle cry of the War of 1812. Commodore Perry defeated the British fleet in the battle of Lake Erie in 1813 and the battles moved away from Fort Detroit and Frenchtown. The war ended in 1815 and settlers began returning to Frenchtown.

The French were mostly farmers with little or no formal education. They were not concerned with developing the potential of the war-torn village. Americans coming from the east quickly saw the opportunity for growth and profit for the town that was on the western end of Lake Erie and the gateway to the west. They saw the growth that took place in the villages of the east and saw the same opportunities in Frenchtown. They also saw that its location was an advantage that villages and cities in the east did not have.

It did not take long for early settlers to notice that goods could move from east to west and any type of seafaring vessel could make the trip to Buffalo and return with goods for trade, barter or sale. The first trading post on the north side of the river gave way to stores on the south side. The first ships brought purchased goods from Buffalo and sold them to the growing number of settlers. Since Frenchtown was new and had limited resources, the goods were in high demand. The East also needed products that were in short supply there, namely farm goods. A booming trade developed between the farmers of Frenchtown and the east on every type of vessel that would float. Mail was arriving to the village weekly by horseback and covered wagon. Included with the mail were newspapers from the larger cities on a delayed delivery. The desire for news made the timing right for a first newspaper as the city became known as **Monroe, Michigan**. *The Michigan Sentinel* was one of the first two newspapers published in the territory. Monroe was fortunate to have Edward Ellis as its first journalist in 1821. Mr. Ellis brought a press and other equipment with him from Buffalo and both he and his paper were well-received. Mr. Ellis was one of the early American businessmen to come to Monroe. News of the outside world and the government would be available for the first time and the settlers supported the paper with advertising and subscriptions.

A historic event was taking place in New York as reported in the newspapers that would fuel the imagination of the people in Monroe. The publication of the newspaper in Monroe and the completion of the Erie Canal took place at the same time. Proposed in 1808 and completed in 1825, the Canal linked the waters of Lake Erie in the west to the Hudson River in the east. In order to open the country west of the Appalachian Mountains to settlers and also offer a cheap and safe way to carry produce to market, Governor Dewitt Clinton proposed the construction of a canal in 1808.

However, it was not until July 4, 1817, that Governor Clinton finally broke ground for the construction of the Canal. In those early days, it was often sarcastically referred to as "Clinton's Big Ditch." When finally completed on October 26, 1825, it was the engineering marvel of its day. It included 18 aqueducts to carry the canal over ravines and rivers, and 83 locks, with a rise of 568 feet from the Hudson River to Lake Erie. It was 4 feet deep and 40 feet wide, and floated boats carrying 30 tons of freight.

The new settlers from the east who had followed the progress of the Canal saw no reason why the River Raisin could not be straightened and made into a major port in the west, and the dream of the river canal in Monroe was born. It would take fifteen years and hundreds of thousands of dollars for that dream to become a reality. That vision of the future did not slow the activities of the day. Pioneers

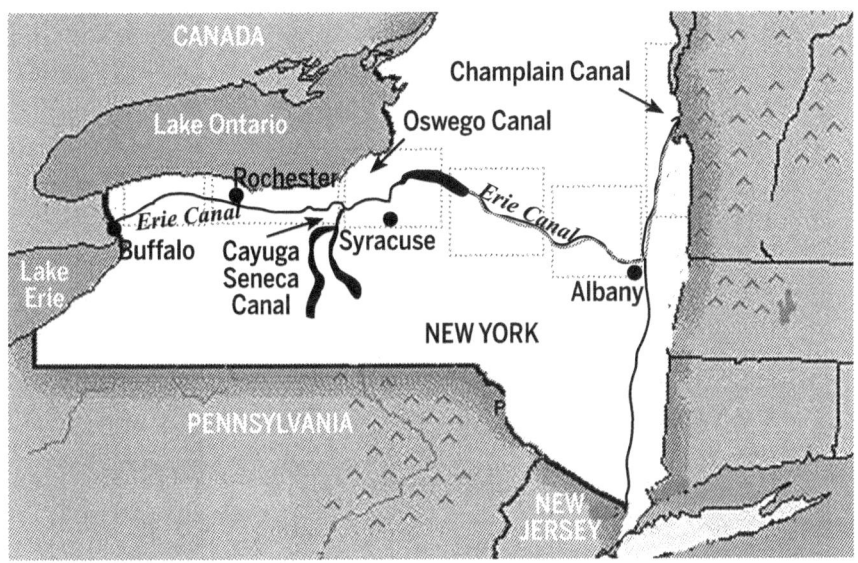

New route to Lake Erie

could safely travel through New York on the waterway with little fear from the Indians. Early Americans could continue west on Lake Erie to Monroe. They could remain in Michigan or continue west where there were opportunities to explore and fortunes to be made.

The following article later appeared in the *Advocate* describing the growth that took place from 1820 to 1836.

"The sale of property in our village continues unabated, and sales thus far obtain the same high prices of the preceding two weeks; and we may truly say lots have risen considerably within the last week, inasmuch as none can be purchased at former prices.

Many landholders in town have refused one hundred per cent advance on last week's purchases. Farms a little below the village, and bordering on the river, have risen about eighty per cent. The Stuart farm, originally containing one hundred and fifty acres, has been sold (or a considerable part of it). Sixteenths (of an acre) were a few days ago at $566.00; they are now selling readily for $1,000.00 and $1,200.00. Lots near the land have been selling at $30.00 per front foot, and these lots are one mile below the village. I do not know of one individual making a purchase of a village lot at $2,000.00 less than two weeks ago, which now is worth $6,000.00 or *an advance of three hundred per cent. Another who paid $9,000.00 for a block of village lots, about the same time, for which he had been offered $17,000.00 and refused. The amount of the sale for this week is about $55,000.00. It had been thought that the cheering intelligence relative to the passing of our ship canal bill in Congress had caused this rise in property in our village, what speaks loudly for our place is the great amount of general business doing here at present.*

We notice, the other day, the erection of 20 to 30 new buildings in Monroe; and this in the heart of winter. Monroe has a population now of about three thousand, and supports twenty-eight dry goods stores, fourteen groceries, two hardware shops, three cabinet shops, five hotels, etc.

A Village

Early Frenchtown had one street along the north side of the river called Water Street, later renamed Elm Street. Water Street began east of the settlement with old smokehouses, grist mills, distilleries and trapper sheds. Later, log houses dotted the northern riverbank. South Monroe Street replaced Kentucky and became the stagecoach route to Ohio. The settlement was beginning to expand. A charter was given to the settlement in 1827 and Monroe officially became a village. The village saw a need to lay out a street plan, as more settlers were arriving. The settlers used the New York model for Monroe. The east-west streets were to be named after presidents and prominent local families: Harrison, Adams, Washington, Navarre, Jerome and Bacon. The north-south streets were named for military men: Macomb, Winchester, Scott. Numbers were used as the city grew: 1st, 2nd and 3rd. A greater number of American settlers began coming to the area and slowly the south side of the river became more populated.

The Settlement of Frenchtown becomes Monroe

The county received its name in 1817 when the Michigan territory received a visit from President Monroe. The county was named in his honor with the village of Monroe as its center. The village of Monroe was on the south side of the river and Frenchtown on the north. The John Anderson trading post was at the center of Frenchtown near Anderson Road running north and south, which would later become North Monroe Street. A stockade and a Catholic Church were west on Water Street. A toll bridge was constructed near Anderson and Water Roads and for a fee of two cents, you could cross the river to the area where the English speaking settlers would later locate. The Monroe Street bridge was built in 1827 and replaced the original toll bridge. As the settlers explored the river, they found that the river flowed west for 175 miles. A few short miles to the southeast on the New England or Yankee side, as the Indians called it, the river emptied into what became known as LaPlaisance Bay. With the new bridge, the ease of transportation connected the two sides of the river into a growing community. Settlers would cluster, build and farm in areas where they shared a common language with their neighbors: German, French and English. Neighborhoods were being established as the growth continued with the arrival of new

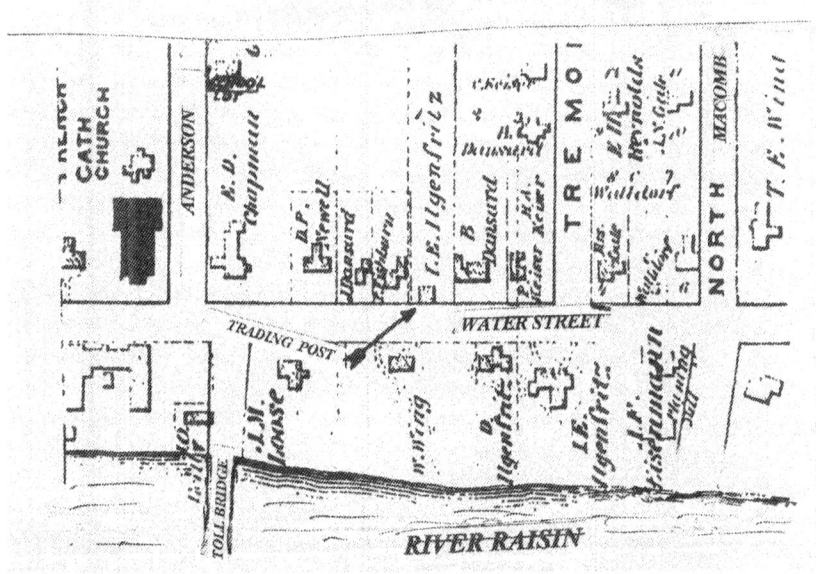

Early map of Frenchtown

Americans. A main street with wood buildings and wood sidewalks was built where Washington Street is now located.

The early trail or road south was Kentucky Street which led to LaPlaisance Road and LaPlaisance Bay. It was also the old road south to Toledo.

LaPlaisance Bay

The River Raisin flows from west to east. It is a narrow river emptying into LaPlaisance Bay, then Lake Erie. The river was almost a trickling brook by late summer, rising slightly with the fall rains and freezing to a glassy surface in the winter. The ice broke with devastating force in the spring, followed by rising waters and flooding along the banks, only to see the cycle repeat itself. The long winding river was home to Indians and wild game prior to the frontier days. The river did not empty into Lake Erie but rather into a large marsh without any direct access into the lake.

Lake traffic had to transfer passengers and cargo to flatbottom boats enroute to the city.

As new maps showed that it would be much easier to travel west by ship along Lake Erie from Buffalo rather than the hazardous 250 mile stage coach ride, new pioneers and adventurers began coming to LaPlaisance Bay.

Captain Luther Harvey, born in Burlington, Vermont, in 1789, owned the first sailing vessel which traveled between Monroe and Buffalo. This boat carried many of the enterprising men from the east who opened the gateway to the west in Monroe and began building the city. The Captain was also an early settler of Frenchtown, where he operated a tavern in 1815 with his family. He continued sailing until 1821 and was an eyewitness to the Battle of Lake Erie in 1815.

In 1825, a group of new settlers from the east would put Monroe on the map when they formed the LaPlaisance Bay Harbor Company. They saw that the ships from the east were coming to the bay in a disorganized manner. They purchased land near the bay and formed the company, which held its first annual meeting on June 2, 1825.

The new directors were Alcott C. Chapman, Charles Noble, Levi S. Humphrey, Oliver Johnson and Harry Conant. John Anderson joined the next year. Levi S. Humphrey was named president; Edward D. Ellis, secretary: Oliver Johnson, treasurer. The first port of Monroe was established and organized commerce began for the fledgling community. Agriculture in southeastern Michigan was flourishing with produce, corn and wheat. The mill of Miler and Germain processed the wheat into flour, shipping 200 barrels to New York from their mill in the village. This was the first major shipment from Monroe, as the super fine white flour was well-received in the East and the fame of Monroe and LaPlaisance Bay began to spread.

General Levi Humphrey was born in Vermont in 1797 and came to Monroe in 1823. He was a stagecoach driver prior to coming to Monroe. He specialized in breeding fine horses and was landlord of the Humphrey Hotel. Charles Noble was born 1797 in Williamstown, Massachusetts. He graduated from college in 1815 with a law degree and came to Monroe in 1818. He was postmaster from 1824 to 1828 and also practiced law. Harry Conant was born in Mansfield, Connecticut, in 1790, then moved to Middlebury, Vermont, in 1801 where he studied medicine. He came to Monroe in 1820 as a doctor. Oliver Johnson was born in Harrington, Connecticut, in 1784 and came to Monroe in 1816. He was a lawyer by profession, but established a store on Front and Washington Streets and became one of the early merchants in Monroe. Alcott C. Chapman was born in Pittsfield, Massachusetts, in 1793. He came to Monroe in 1813 and established a hotel in Monroe, which was the largest in the state before he died at the age of 38. Captain Henry Smith, Superintendent of Governmental Works, was authorized by the government to oversee the development of the River Raisin Canal and a new port on the river.

Ansel Strong ventured to Michigan in 1828 at the age of 26. He became well aware of what had taken place in the settlement over the past few years. Not able to afford the price of land in Monroe, he ventured on to Jackson, Michigan where he purchased farmland and also married. He returned to Norfolk, New York, to gather his possessions there and inform his brother of the opportunities in

Michigan. He returned to his new home and bride, never to venture east again.

George W. Strong followed his brother to Monroe in 1832 and immediately began working on the piers for the breakwater at Raisin Point for Captain Smith. He lived and worked in Monroe for the next 60 years. During those 60 years he would become one of the greatest pioneer names of historic Old Monroe and the builder and owner of the Strong Hotel.

President James Monroe
*The county received its name in 1817 when the Michigan territory
received a visit from President Monroe.*

Chapter 4- **Village to City and Captain George W. Strong**

The trip across Vermont, then upstate New York to Norfolk was more stressful than George W. Strong, his family and Ansel Strong expected. The summer rains, with only a wagon for shelter, made for long days and nights. The trails turned to mud and ruts, requiring everyone to slip, slosh, push and pull the wagon and team. There was no way to remove the mud until arriving at the next creek or river. There were many Indian sightings, few settlements and very harsh terrain. News of roaming bands of Indians required changes in routes, making the journey more difficult. The most unsettling was the discomfort of the two small children. New to child rearing, concern for the health and safety of George, age three, and Helen, age one, introduced the young couple to the stress of parenthood. There were times when they wondered if they had made the right decision, but they never considered returning to Vermont.

Having survived the wilderness, the Strongs arrived in Norfolk, New York, weary but in a positive frame of mind. With next to no possessions, they began to make provisions for a new home. Their first lodging was at a tavern for travelers, which seemed luxurious after weeks in the wilderness traveling along Indian trails. The town of one hundred people was fair size for that period in America. Work was available in the saw mills, grist mill or farms, and George chose the saw mill, knowing that he would one day need to build a home. As conditions improved, Hannah put the grueling trip from Vermont behind her and fell into the routine of a pioneer homemaker.

Ansel Strong joined George and Hannah in 1829, returning from the Michigan Territory with tales of opportunity and profit that sparked the spirit of adventure in George W. Strong. George knew that Norfolk would be another small settlement in the years ahead, similar to Chelsea and Stockbridge. He knew some day he would be moving on and would find what he was best suited for. Hannah was to be a mother for the third time in 1827 and a son, Thomas, was born later that year. Priorities once again changed and George and Ansel set about building a permanent log home for the family. Dreams would be set aside for George with the new addition to the family. Ansel had persuaded George to return to Michigan with him in 1829 and George was ready, had Hannah not been expecting again. Ansel returned to Michigan in 1830 and George and Hannah were blessed with twin sons, Alonzo and Thurlow.

Letters continued to arrive from Ansel, and George was convinced to venture on to Michigan. The children were older and healthy and George had set enough aside for Hannah that he was once again ready to make the move west and hopefully fulfill his destiny. Hannah knew that she had delayed the move for six years, but the day would soon come when it would be time to relocate. This time, George was to make the 533 mile passage to Michigan alone. His goal was to insure that the family would be comfortable when later arriving in Michigan. The older children were eight and seven years old, while the twins were two when George prepared to leave the family behind and venture to Michigan. George W. Strong left Norfolk, New York, in 1832 seeking to fulfill his destiny.

The journey west began along the St. Lawrence River, then on the shores of Lake Ontario to Buffalo. George made the trip on horseback with only a sack containing few possessions.

His excitement began to build when he found that everyone in Buffalo knew of Frenchtown. Buffalo was the first large town that he had visited since Glastonbury, which he barely remembered. The journey continued for George Strong traveling by water from the port at Buffalo with its increasing number of vessels bound for Monroe, Detroit or the Maumee River. Monroe was the least desirable location for passenger travel and was better known as a commercial shipping destination. Many of the early settlers first went to Detroit, then on to Monroe by land. George was fascinated by the sailing vessels as he sailed along the shoreline of Lake Erie, passing Put In Bay, where the battle of Lake Erie took place and then veered north nearing the western end of Lake Erie enroute to the more popular port at Detroit. Monroe could be seen in the distance. Monroe was well-known in the East with its port at the River Raisin to be completed in the future. Detroit was both a growing city and a pass-through point for travelers heading west. The port in Detroit was larger than George had expected and travelers were surprised at the number of Detroiters who spoke French.

The last leg of the journey for George was to travel to Monroe by stagecoach. The ride south seemed endless, although it lasted only six hours in good dry weather. The road led through level, wooded country and was rather dull for those seeking a scenic trip with Indians along the roadside. Passengers could see that the soil was rich, fat and black as lush vegetation grew at a distance. The coach would slow as it traveled over several muddy creeks, then regain its momentum as dust and speed were synonymous. The lake to the east was not visible through the forests but the east winds brought the scent of the warm waters to the passengers. Reaching Frenchtown, the coach traveled along Water Street across the bridge over the River Raisin and arrived at its destination on Front Street in the town of Monroe. George W. Strong arrived in Monroe like most males traveling alone, with one large duffle bag containing personal items, clothes and shoes, and he stood on Monroe soil for the first time in 1832. The downtown buildings were not what one would expect, as they seemed to be scattered here and there in no organized manner. The town had doubled in size in the last year and there were 150 buildings in the area with a population of about 1,600. A traveler's first thought was that these old buildings should be burned down and the town built anew. There were two grist mills immediately in the center of town, a woolen factory, an iron foundry, several saw mills, a chair factory, a tannery and a general store. The river afforded ample water power for the residences and machinery.

The first stop for George Strong was at the Monroe House owned by Joseph Loranger on the corner of Front and Monroe Streets. This would be his home for the next few months. On his second day in Monroe, George Strong purchased a horse from Levi Humphrey suitable for riding and pulling a wagon and then prepared to meet with Captain Harry Smith. Captain Smith was born in Stillwater, New York, and was two years older than George. Captain Smith graduated from West Point in 1816 and served actively in the military before coming to Monroe in 1832, the same year as Strong. The federal government had approved Monroe's request for funds to construct the River Raisin Canal, thinking that a port in southeastern Michigan would have military value. Captain Smith was sent to administer the funding and oversee the work being done.

George knew from information gathered back East that the person he needed to contact was Captain Harry Smith. On the second day in Monroe, George Strong furnished Captain Smith a letter of introduction and was immediately hired to work under contract on the breakwater near LaPlaisance Bay and the river. His good sense for business proved to be advantageous. Strong quickly determined to seize the opportunity at LaPlaisance Bay, taking a contract to build a breakwater at the mouth of the old river. The early settlers were the first to use LaPlaisance Bay for trade with cities along Lake Erie. Warehouses and docking arrangements were made on the banks near what is now known as Bolles Harbor. A land route by wagon and a crude rail system were developed to get the goods to and from the town. LaPlaisance Bay itself was quite large and was one of nature's little treasures.

George had a fondness for the water and life on the river. He had known little else since he left Glastonbury as a youth. He saw the River Raisin as a manageable river of opportunity. He also felt that he had more river experience than many of the businessmen who were already there. He proceeded to dedicate himself to his tasks for he was now a man on a mission, and he had finally tasted his destiny.

Work on the breakwater was to take its toll on the men of the time. Michigan and the West were being scourged by cholera and, like many others, George Strong became ill. He was afflicted with the disease, but because of his healthy condition, was able to survive as were most of the white settlers. The Indians who contracted the disease were not as fortunate and the Indian population was adversely affected. Strong found that he was better suited to succeed in Monroe than a number of younger men because of his good health, education and business background. Once the cholera had passed, he was again in excellent health. LaPlaisance Bay was an active and busy business location although still somewhat disorganized. The larger boats anchored offshore and smaller flatbottom boats brought

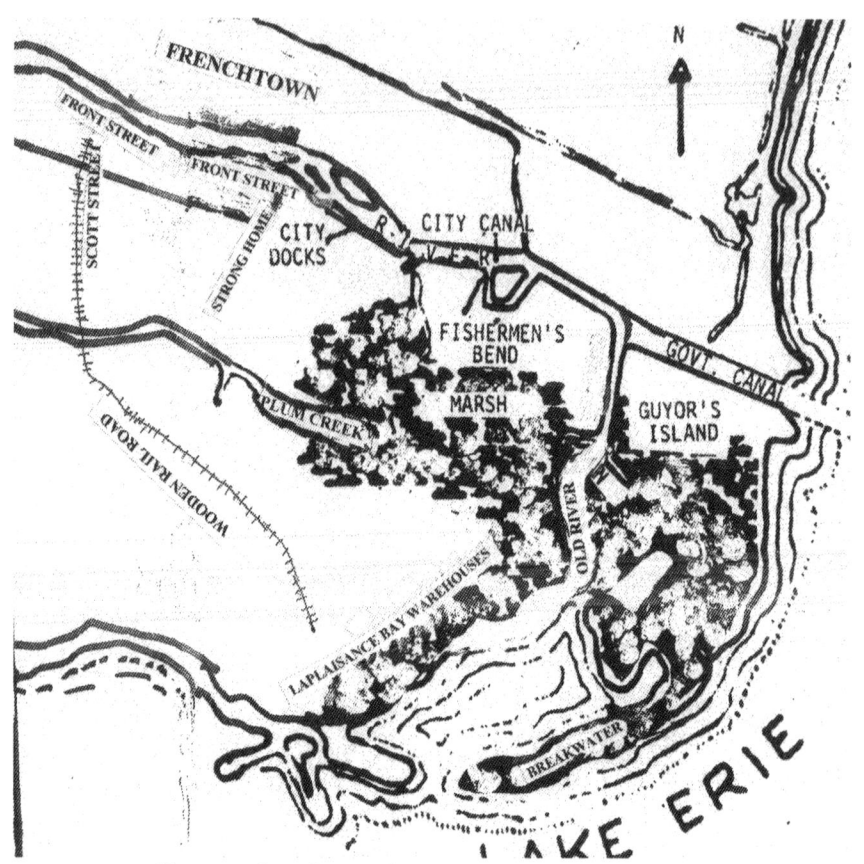

Bolles Harbor bay inlet on a map from approx. 1832

the cargo to the docks of the LaPlaisance Bay Harbor Company. The winding River Raisin and Plum Creek emptied into the bay. Guyor's Island, Kauslers Island, Sandy Isle, Du Bois Isle, Fox Isle, Crow Isle, Wood Duck Isle and Willow Isle were small, above-lake, level land areas along the river and in the bay.

Cattails, rice grass, bull rushes, lotus beds and trees could be found throughout the marsh. Every type of fish and wildlife indigenous to Michigan inhabited the marsh in plentiful supply. The open water area in the bay was deep enough for only flatbottom boats. There was an inlet for access into the bay and the less desirable old river channel. The River Raisin traveled east from the city, twisted and

59

turned, then followed a sharp curve south into the bay before it emptied into Lake Erie.

The people of early Monroe thought the river would be of no commercial use with its shallow outlet, until they heard of the progress of the Erie Canal. The possibility of straightening out the river became an obsession and in 1834, the town fathers petitioned Congress for a canal which would provide a direct route for the river into the lake. Meanwhile, work was being planned to improve LaPlaisance Bay and the River.

If George Strong had been a common laborer, he could have worked at the River Raisin Project as long as he desired. The work on the piers and the river would go on for years. This was not Mr. Strong's style. He preferred doing things his way rather than being directed by others. He was one to follow his dreams and not the dreams of others. He completed the contract on the breakwater with the government, and then severed his business connection, but not his friendship with the Captain and the government.

Captain Smith represented Monroe in getting congressional approval for his plan to cut a canal 4,000 feet long and 100 feet wide east to Lake Erie along the north side of Guyor's Island. The plan called for dredging and construction at a cost of nearly $100,000. A good sense for business proved to be advantageous as George Strong determined that LaPlaisance Bay and the River Raisin would provide an opportunity for prosperity. The breakwater required building a rock jetty in the shallows where the lake met the bay. It was physically demanding and consisted of moving large rocks from the banks to the bay. It was during the two years under contract that Strong developed a friendship with the equally young and energetic men of the Harbor Company. Humphrey, Nobel, Conant, Johnson and Chapman began a business relationship and friendship with George Strong and shared a grand vision for LaPlaisance Bay. The enthusiasm of these men from the East convinced Strong to make a commitment to Monroe and venture into the shipping business. He was familiar with ships, thanks to his older brother who was a sea captain, among other things. Perhaps the closest friend of Strong was Captain Smith who convinced Strong that the River

Raisin had future potential for commerce. The tireless Mr. Strong then embarked on his first private business venture in Monroe in 1835. He built and ran a fleet of sand scowls or flatbottom boats to bring light loads of freight from vessels anchored in the lake to the docks on the river just east of town. His flatbottom boats on the bay prospered and expanded to meet the demands of the growing trade with the East. This method of transportation was so successful by the time Monroe became a city in 1837, Strong became known as Captain George W. Strong and was in command of a small fleet and an equal number of sailors.

Two of the men that George Strong developed a friendship with in his first year in Monroe were Captain Smith and Dr. R. G. Clark. Captain Smith awarded Strong the contract for the breakwater and Dr. Clark helped in the recovery from cholera. Dr. Clark was so impressed with the young Strong that he went into partnership in building one of the first warehouses on the River. Dr. Clark, who was one of Monroe's first doctors, passed away shortly after. George Strong had made a commitment to Monroe in his first year with the investment in the warehouse. Strong returned to Norfolk, New York, in 1834 and made arrangements to move his wife, Hannah and his five children to Monroe. He settled his affairs, leaving the family comfortable, then returned to Monroe and began building the flatbottom boats that would transfer freight from the lake ships to both the warehouse at LaPlaisance Bay and the river docks. It took only three years for George W. Strong to become a noted and respected businessman in Monroe. His family arrived in Monroe in 1835 with the addition of a new son, William, and Strong began a new pioneer adventure that would last the next fifty-five years in Monroe.

Hannah and Children join George Strong in Monroe

Hannah was thirty-three years old with six children when George made the final commitment to Frenchtown and arranged for his family to join him. They left their home in Norfolk, their friends and most of the goods that they had acquired during thirteen years of marriage. The choices for travel were steamer or stagecoach and the decision was made to travel by stagecoach, which allowed Hannah to bring a few extra items to her new home. She made the trip with one year old William in her arms, along with the other five children ages six to eleven. To Hannah's surprise, she arrived in a community that was changing by the day in 1835. The new Monroe Street Bridge was busy with traffic connecting the old and new part of town. The intersection of Front and Washington was the center of downtown which was only two blocks long. Front Street wound east along the river for about a mile to the river islands, then the dirt road continued to the docks and finally led to the marsh, Guyor's Island and LaPlaisance Bay. Front Street was the commercial highway for Monroe as the goods and travelers entered the settlement from the river docks. George had spent all his life near a river and it was no wonder that the home he had prepared was along Front Street near the River Raisin. Hannah expected a much larger river from the accounts of George's business ventures. When compared to the Connecticut River and other much larger rivers in the East, the River Raisin seemed an oversized creek. It was not a river to be feared.

No sooner had Hannah and the children arrived in Monroe, when Ohio convinced Congress to move the state line north to where it is today and the **Toledo War** started the same year. The citizens of Michigan began gathering in Monroe to take back Toledo with force of arms. Hannah must have wondered what George Strong had gotten her into as she saw the talk of military action begin. No fighting ever took place and the dispute was settled with a compromise resulting in Michigan's boundary including the Upper Peninsula. Hannah was also surprised that unlike her home in the East, not all settlers spoke English. There were a large number of French-speaking people in the community. She was pleased that, like herself, many in Monroe could not read or write, and the merchants and citizens were understanding and offered assistance whenever needed.

The Strong family made their new start in Monroe from very humble beginnings in a pioneer fashion frame home. George was conservative and principled when it came to spending on himself and his family. He could have built a large home in the village and made payments with returns from his business. He chose instead to build up his capital and live modestly in a home near the river.

George planned the arrival of the family before the Independence Day celebration of 1835. George had attended the celebrations the past two years and felt remorse that his wife and children could not be there with him. Those were the occasions, along with New Year's Day, when their absence was most difficult. The first major family social event began with a parade led by the city band starting at the Macomb Street house and proceeding to the Episcopal Church. The choir sang the anthem and the Rev. Center led a Christian prayer honoring God and country. Mr. Brayman read a patriotic poem accompanied by the band. The Declaration of Independence was read by Mr. Howe, followed by a talk on national character. After the ceremony, everyone proceeded back to the Macomb House for an excellent dinner prepared by Mr. Chamberlin and the evening continued with toasts of everyone's fine wines. This was Hannah and the children's introduction to Monroe and no one could have been happier than George Strong.

The first year was a busy one for Hannah as she made the new home comfortable for the family. She took charge of the domestic needs, allowing George to devote full attention to his business ventures. She also insured that the children continued their Christian upbringing by becoming active in the Methodist Church, which George also patronized. The first year ended joyfully as the family celebrated New Year's Day. One of the pleasant customs of the times which continued for over a half a century was celebrating the advent of the New Year. It was a special day set aside for visiting friends whom they seldom had a chance to visit except on special occasions. Nearly every home was open to callers who were welcomed with genuine, hearty hospitality which went far to promote friendship among the citizens. As the homes became mansions, tables were laden with everything that could tempt the appetite. Parties of four or five would use a sleigh with sweet silver bells ringing to make the rounds. The evening would end with a public or private dance at Old Exchange or later at the Humphrey House. The New Year custom was probably brought to this country by the Dutch and the Huguenots and became universal around 1790. Never in George's wildest dreams did he ever imagine that one day he would host the New Year's Eve celebration in his luxurious Strong Hotel or that one day it would become the Park Hotel.

The cold Michigan winter was an adjustment for the family. There was much needed quiet time with the short days and long dark nights. George would help home-school the children and read the newspapers thoroughly. Winter sports on the ice and snow comprised the fun time for the family. As the year ended and the cold winter passed, the ice began disappearing from the lake and bay, George Strong was thinking of the coming year.

The year 1835 was the beginning of what became a golden year for Monroe. The legislature had granted a charter constituting Monroe a city and the first election for Mayor and Alderman had taken place. The population was about 3,000 and the optimistic citizens expected that to expand to 10,000 by 1840. The state had approved a railroad to cross the state from Monroe to New Buffalo, appropriating $100,000 for the project. One hundred new homes were being constructed around the city, and Macomb Street was to be extended to the north on the Frenchtown side of the river. Front Street on the south side of the river was to be widened and straightened to meet business needs. Expectations were so high that Monroe's future growth was expected to make it the largest city west of Buffalo, NY, and one day the River Raisin the largest port on the lake. Prosperity in the city aided Captain Strong in entering Great Lakes shipping in 1836 when he built the *Elvira Smith.* The ship was named after the wife of Captain Smith who remained a close friend of George Strong. One year after arriving in Monroe, Smith built the most stately home in Monroe on E. Water Street (now E. Elm) with its large white pillars. The home was to maintain the status to which the family was accustomed. His wife, Elvira, was a learned woman from the East and stood out among the women of the times. She was the eldest daughter of Judge Jabez H. Foster, a prominent citizen in Watertown, New York. George associated Elvira with his grandparents the Stockings in Glastonbury. She represented the life that his mother often mentioned and the family left behind when his father left Glastonbury for Vermont. Hannah, who was the opposite of Elvira, was not comfortable with the friendship, but accepting. George Strong had lent a helping hand in building the Smith home and unlike George, Captain Smith believed in stature and prestige. The house was next to the home of John Anderson who resided on the corner west of the Anderson Street Bridge. Elvira lived in the home for many years after the death of Smith, who was promoted to Major. The house later became known as the Ilgenfritz home.

Patriot War

The close relationship with Captain Smith and Elvira resulted in Captain Strong's involvement in the Patriot War in 1837. The Patriot War was not newsworthy but it did involve Captain Strong. Michigan became a state on January 26, 1837. A year later, January 1838, the militia, under state organization, was in active operations. Although it was not a major campaign, this war did furnish some action for the soldiers. The Patriot War was brought about by residents of both upper Canada and the United States, of Irish descent or birth, and citizens who had moved to Canada. These Patriots, as they called themselves, planned to detach the peninsula lying between the Michigan frontier and the Niagara frontier from Canada and attach it to the United States. Their base of operations was located in Michigan and they were organized into secret groups known as Hunters Lodges.

In the early winter of 1837-38, straggling parties of armed men waited along the border for ice to form on the St. Clair River. This was the route over which they planned to enter Canada, unfurl their flag, and establish a temporary government in rebellion against the British crown. The attempt was foiled by a detachment of Canadians. Their arms and ammunition were taken back to Detroit. In the latter part of December 1837, the Patriots used a small steamboat to cross into Canada and landed a short distance above Windsor. They marched down to the village opposite Detroit and in the engagement that followed, the Battle of Windsor, a number of men on both sides were killed or wounded. The Patriots scattered to the woods. A plot was then discovered to capture the United States Arsenal at Dearborn and take possession of the arms stored there. To thwart this action, a company of the Michigan Militia was assigned guard duty at the arsenal. The excitement continued through 1838; however, the "Battle of Windsor" is considered the closing of the war. This led to the establishment of the State Guards.

The Patriot War did play a small part in the events taking place in Monroe. The citizens thought the skirmish had very little merit. Captain Smith, who was involved in the war, approached Captain Strong to store guns and ammunition in his warehouse to assist the Arsenal in Dearborn. This proved to be ill-fated on Captain Strong's part. Just as the short war ended, the warehouse was raided and the guns and ammunition were stolen by the Patriots. Following the war, Captain Strong continued building ships and increased his business on the Great Lakes. In five short years in Monroe, Strong had become one of the main contributors to the management of the fledgling town.

Monroe becomes a City

By 1836, the new settlers from the east who had established themselves at LaPlaisance Bay were becoming involved in the civic affairs of the community.

Noble, Conant, Johnson and Ellis were among the men who involved themselves in the process of Monroe becoming a city. *The Monroe Times* owned by E. G. Morton officially reported on April 6, 1837, that Monroe had become a city.

Monroe met the requirements of the State and determined its boundaries, which included the River Raisin, Noble Avenue, the Alexander Robert farm and LaPlaisance Bay. The city was then divided into five wards and a process was set in place to elect officials. The first election was held and the more established residents were placed in the position of responsibility. Tax policies, ordinances and all matters required to manage the city were beginning to be defined.

One of the important matters in that first year that required city involvement was an update on the River Raisin Harbor - Ship Canal. The city was advised that piles were to be driven on both sides of the river, ten feet apart for a distance of about three thousand feet. Caps were secured on 2,020 feet of pilings and sheet-piling driven behind the caps. It was reported that the lake levels rose two feet and eight inches during the year causing accidents and construction delays. Additional workers were needed in order to complete the project on schedule by 1840. Projected additional costs included $15,500 for dredging, $16,720 for excavating, $14,700 for pier work and $10,626 for labor. The report was accepted with enthusiasm by the Council and citizens of Monroe knew that 1840 would begin a new era for Monroe.

A New Home for the Strong Family

Three years after the family arrived in 1838, George purchased a parcel of land from Chester Stewart near the river docks for $10 to build the first family home. The site that George chose for the structure was toward the end of Front Street, near the River Raisin. George was patient and waited for the location that suited his future business interests at a price that could not be resisted. The activity on LaPlaisance Bay made this an active area and the location was very familiar to Strong. He knew that it would be important to the growth of Monroe. It was here that he would begin to establish himself as one of Monroe's top businessmen.

With the help of his boys, he built a large frame home of wood on the sizeable parcel of land that he purchased. It was the type of home that was being built in Monroe, replacing the early pioneer homes. The six children were between four and thirteen years old when they moved into their new home. Living along the river in its natural state with a marsh a mile down the path and the center of town two miles to the west was much different from the farm they left back East. The first tasks included making the home suitable for everyone. Chores were given to the children for summer and winter. Gathering firewood, tending the animals and garden, and exploring made up the day. The boys fished and hunted, both as a new pastime and to provide game for meals. A short time after the newness became routine; more time was spent in town. Hannah had finally realized the dream of owning a home that she knew would be permanent.

The one thing that did not change as the family moved to their new home was their religious practices. The Strongs were Methodist by birth and George introduced the family to Rev. Triggs and Rev. Preziker shortly after the family arrived in Monroe. Every Sunday, the family would put on their best clothes and ride the horse-drawn wagon to the church on Monroe Street. The family was quickly well-known, but not considered prosperous when they arrived in 1835. The Fourth Quarter Methodist Conference with H. Colelazer presiding was held in Monroe. Church measures were defined and adopted for the community, and both George and Hannah were very interested and involved. Monroe became a "station" and the newly created church was named Wesley Chapel. It would not be called St. Paul's until much later. The Church suffered financial difficulty in 1842 as a result of the panic of 1837. Many of the sermons preached during the time, and appropriate in light of the financial problems of the Church, were on wealth and morality. The citizens had a false sense of wealth due to the inflated value of the land they possessed. The moralists were concerned that people were living beyond their means because of their wealth. People were rich on paper and in their own minds in times of careless speculation and free banking. Some were operating on conduct that was less than upright. The panic of 1837 and 1838 was the result of this abuse and carelessness. Churchgoers were warned not to let this side of human nature persist. A program was put in place to sell church pews in honor of donors in order to raise funds. Well-known names in Monroe were among the members and donors. Along with George Strong were Hon. R. McClelland (Governor), J. Armitage (wool merchant), Livi Humphry (military and business), E. Morton, H. Stone, W. Clarke, J. Morton, F. Winene and E. Reynolds. These men were also among the active businessmen involved in the growth of the city. Four short years after the family arrived in Monroe, George Strong was already successful in his various businesses at the city docks. As the decade was nearing an end, George was one of the most respected citizens of Monroe. He had already achieved more than he thought possible in the earlier years, as he was traveling through the wilderness enroute to Norfolk, New York.

Monroe County Court House.

Chapter 5 - **Progress and George Strong**

The Twilight of LaPlaisance Bay

George W. Strong saw one natural wonder and a river with potential when he arrived in Frenchtown. Nothing in the East came close to the wonders of LaPlaisance Bay. He understood at once why there were so many Indian signs in the area. It was a natural paradise about to become ravaged by progress. Strong easily related to the River Raisin It was not unlike many of the small rivers that carved the landmark all the way to the Atlantic Ocean. The landscape was the same but it would change, along with the men who would develop it.

Time and nature clashed at LaPlaisance Bay and a transformation took place at both the Bay and in George Strong. The growth of shipping and warehousing was complemented by the change in the men associated with LaPlaisance Bay. The public perceived George Strong as someone they should know and respect. Success transformed private family men to public figures of power. The evolving process of maturity and success took place in Strong. Marriage, then the first child, followed by a second, then twins demanded focus and commitment. George was consumed by being a provider and a father as the newlyweds began their travels in the East. He, Hannah and the children were never apart. Everything he did was for them. Every cry of the infant children was a new and impacting emotion. Concerns of Hannah made George look to himself long and hard. He was still a Strong. That, he could not escape. Despite having a family of seven, he knew there was something he was destined for elsewhere. It was out there and he had to find it.

All the beauty of LaPlaisance Bay was slow to counter the loneliness that Strong had felt when he left his family behind to venture west to Frenchtown. It was the unlimited opportunities of the Bay that would comfort him until the family would reunite.

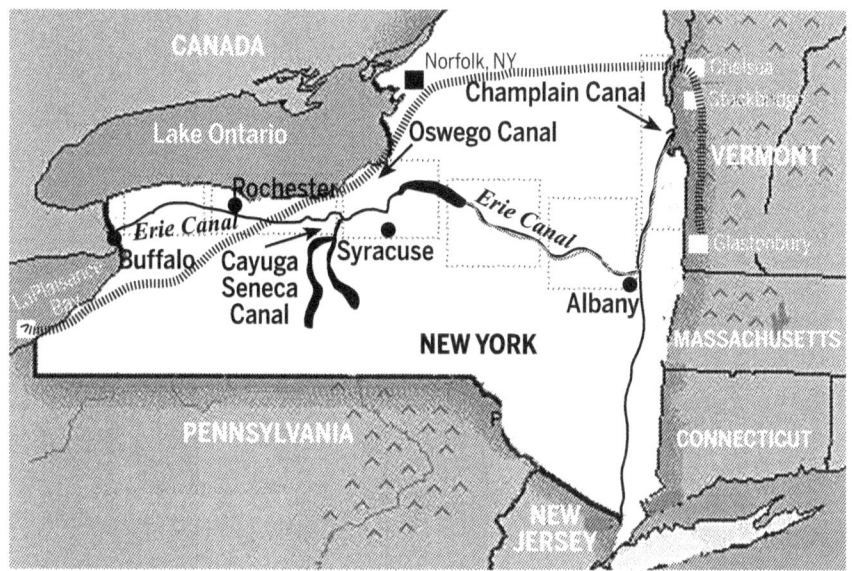

LaPlaisance Bay - End of a Long Journey

George W. Strong met Captain Smith his second day in Frenchtown and a transition began from what he was to what he would become. The chemistry was perfect. Smith and Strong immediately related to each other and fed off their common dreams. Strong had been in Monroe only two days and had one long conversation with Captain Smith when their friendship was cemented. The Captain was only two years older than Strong but shared common experiences.

Henry Smith was born in Stillwater, New York, the son of a doctor. He graduated from West Point and boasted of a military career that included Indian fighting and traveling as far as Fort Snelling, between St. Paul and Minneapolis. The Erie Canal, cutting through New York, convinced the military that there was a strategic value in building canals to improve river access for the future defense of the Union. He was ordered by the government to take charge of the work on the harbor at LaPlaisance Bay and the River.

George Strong remembered Glastonbury, Connecticut, his birth place, and the growing settlements and cities along Connecticut River. He could foresee a city one day in Frenchtown. Plans to connect the River Raisin to Lake Erie were set in motion shortly before George Strong arrived at Frenchtown. A bill was passed in both houses of

River Raisin before City Canal

Congress appropriating $15,000 to begin work dredging the large sand bar that diverted the river into LaPlaisance Bay. With the War of 1812 fresh in their minds, the citizens wanted the protection for the commercial value of the port. The Government quickly approved the funding for its military potential. The River Raisin could be a military port defending the eastern end of the lakes and the gateway to the West. The nearby Maumee River in Ohio could not compete at the time because of the large swamp at its mouth. George Strong knew that Frenchtown, soon to be named Monroe, would benefit from the immense trade and commerce that must flow west.

The young man that once considered law, medicine and music, had found his calling in shipping. The flat bottom fleet at the bay had been very profitable and after only three years in Michigan, he was ready for bigger and better ventures. Great Lakes shipping, as great a challenge as it seemed a few years earlier, was the next opportunity that lured Strong from the tame river traffic. Strong, with his family remaining in Norfolk, New York, until 1834, enjoyed hours of conversation with Captain Smith discussing their experiences and expectations. Strong so respected the insight from the Captain, that he made a commitment to the Bay and River at once. With nothing but time on his hands, and a family back in Norfolk, he worked like a man possessed, preparing for the day his family would join him.

The two men were also different in many ways. Captain Smith was outgoing and displayed the status and prestige of his position in the community. Shortly after arriving in Monroe, he proceeded to build one of the most stately homes in the community. George Strong, a more private and conservative person, helped construct the Smith mansion while living in a very modest pioneer dwelling near the bay. The two men were bound by ideas and imagination rather than lifestyle.

Strong and Smith also differed in their choice of spouses. Smith married Miss Elvira Lorraine Foster, eldest daughter of Judge Jabez H. Foster, a prominent citizen of Watertown, New York. Elvira was an intelligent, well-bred lady from the East and the Smiths had two children when they arrived in Monroe. George Strong, on the other hand, married the daughter of a rural family in Vermont. She had little formal learning. Elvira and George developed a special relationship and she, with Captain Smith, encouraged George to be aggressive in following his plans for the Bay and the River.

Dredge Used in Constructing City Canal at Monroe

George W. Strong's comfort level with rivers and lakes made him fearless in building a fleet of flat-bottom boats shortly after completing work on the breakwater.

The river harbor was years away and the Bay was a busy place with great warehouses and wharves being built. LaPlaisance Bay was reaching its commercial peak when Strong saw that change was looming over the distant horizon. He initiated a new concept in shipping by building the *Water Witch*. This flat-bottom steamer would carry freight and passengers from offshore at the bay up the old riverbed to the river's end near the city along Front Street. The steamer traveled from the lake, zigzagged through the marsh to the

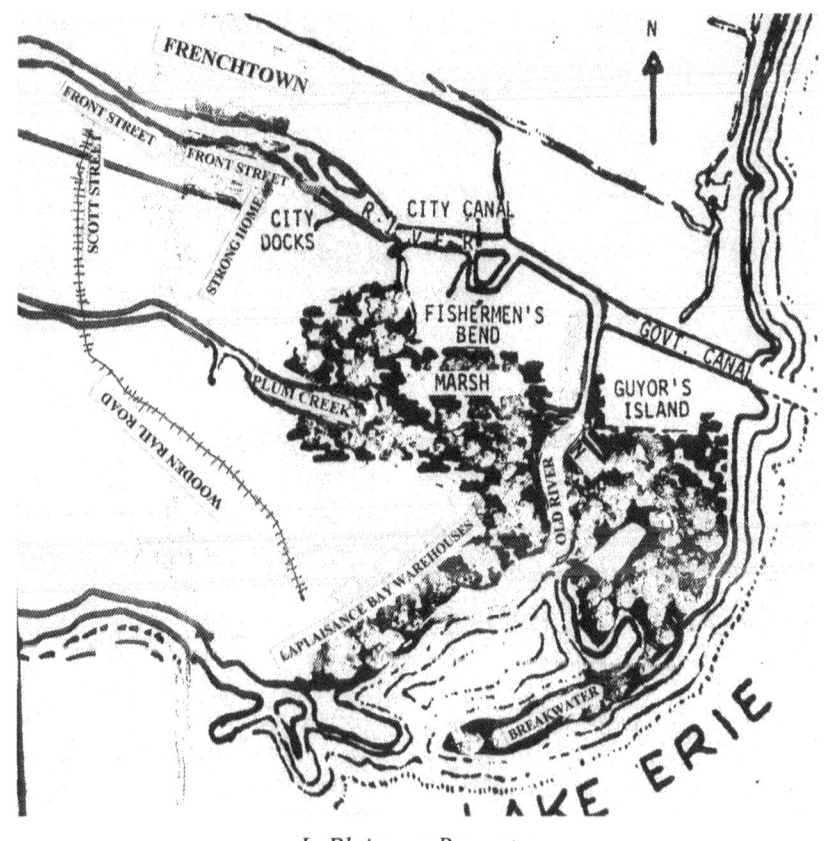

LaPlaisance Bay entrance
to old River Raisin

river outlet, following the river to the docks near Front and Scott Streets where the railroad ended.

The businessmen of the city wondered if Strong was doomed to failure with his bold venture. However, they soon found out that George W. Strong had established a new water route to the city and it would be LaPlaisance Bay, that in time, would be doomed.

He had been in Monroe for only five years when he began to shape the events that would take place in the city. Shipping and inland commerce were becoming more regulated, as were the railroads. Competition was a new menace that Captain Strong and those involved with the Bay had to contend with.

Captain Strong led the captains at LaPlaisance Bay, including Captain Luther Harvey, Joseph Sterling, William Noble, Fredrick Walldorf, John Burch, Thomas Pleus, Stalham Wing, Tunis Van Brunt, Fifield & Sterling, William Studdeford, G. Morris, J. J.

THE CANAL, MONROE, MICH.

Godfroy and S. Dustin in the transition to the river. The activity at the Bay began to phase out as the government channel was completed, resulting in shipping activity moving to the River Raisin.

Year by year, the bay would become a more ghostly sight with abandoned warehouses as the railroad activity moved to the river along Front Street. George Strong was looking to the River Raisin and did not look back as LaPlaisance Bay became a part of Historic Monroe.

The River Canal

The Monroe businessmen were driven to build a large class steam boat that cost about $45,000 to run between Buffalo and Monroe. The first launch in Monroe took place in 1833. Citizens came from miles around to witness the event. A brass band added color to the occasion. The selection of the name was changed from *Diane,* then to *Tecumseh* and finally settled on *Revenge*.

It was during this time that George Strong was taken by a mild case of cholera. He had been working long hours and irregularly fed himself and rested. In his weakened condition and exposure to workers at the bay and river, he was slowed by the illness. Care during his illness came from Elvira Smith and Dr. R. G. Clark. His special friendship with Elvira continued. In her, he saw qualities of his mother. She reflected the learning and culture of the East and did not totally submit to her husband. He could relate to her in a manner different from his wife, Hannah. Hannah was fascinated by his learning and the fact that he was a descendant of Elder John Strong. Unlike Smith, who was very disciplined and predictable, George Strong had the pioneer spirit and sought adventure and risk with enthusiasm. Elvira, along with Dr. Clark, tended to Strong daily, resulting in a speedy recovery. As a token of gratitude, he would name his next ship after her. The young man also impressed Dr. Clark. Strong spoke freely of his plans for the River Raisin to the extent that Dr. Clark was willing to invest in his dreams. George W. Strong discovered that he was acquiring power in Monroe. Wealthy businessmen were willing to finance his business ventures. What

Strong did not realize, was that with power comes the risk of change in a man.

Following his illness, Captain Strong formed a partnership with Dr. Clark and embarked on building his first Lake Erie ship, the *Elvira Smith*, a flat-bottom steamer; he commissioned her in the same successful business as the flat bottom boats. It was the first light draught small steamer launched in the River Raisin.

New City Canal opens.

He was becoming well-known as Captain Strong when he entered the grain trade between Michigan and Canada from the docks on the river. He next purchased and added the famous 35-ton sloop built earlier, *Revenge*, to his operation and his fame. This naturally opened up other business enterprises and he established a forwarding and commission business. He built a large warehouse at the city docks on the river plus a large general store which sold marine and farming supplies.

When the government work began on the River Raisin Canal,

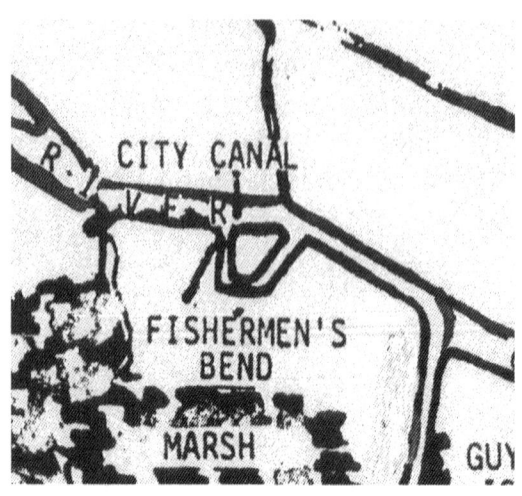

A bend in the river.

the citizens wanted to make improvements on the river by digging what was known as the City Canal. While the excitement ran high in 1839 for the government canal, Captain Strong put in a bid with Henry Campbell to complete the City Canal. Captain Strong and Henry W. Campbell were elected to be the contractors. The Canal required straightening the big bend in the river to shorten the river route by 1300 feet. This was to be a city-financed extension of the government canal. A bond issued for $25,000 was easily passed, but did not readily sell because of financial problems and the panic of 1837.

Wildcat schemes throughout the country and especially in New York, began to collapse and the effect was also felt in Monroe. Monroe had its share of these schemes and when the panic struck, many fortunes were wiped out and business firms were forced into bankruptcy. George W. Strong was known to work best under extreme adversity and had the respect and confidence of his fellow citizens. He was able to weather the panic and continue his operations along LaPlaisance Bay and the River Raisin. Business conditions began to slowly improve but Mr. Campbell had retired and Captain Strong was forced to finish the Canal alone.

The year 1842 was a busy one as the Captain was finishing the work on the City Canal and beginning construction on two new ships. He laid the keels of the steamer *Macomb* and *Helen Strong,* a side-wheeler. He had also made a commitment to the River Raisin Docks by building another larger warehouse there. The following year, both boats were completed. It was an opportunity for his sons to begin their involvement in the family business. The ship was commissioned to run the Monroe to Buffalo route. The *Macomb* serviced travel between Monroe, Detroit and Toledo.

Busy City Canal

Captain George W. Strong was well-established and ready when the canal was completed in 1843. Monroe County and the southern part of the state continued to be blessed by nature. The soil was the richest and most productive in the State. The rainfall and climate made an ideal growing season. Farming was a growing business and there were sufficient workers to yield large crops. The railroad was running from Adrian carrying crops to the docks. Shipments were made daily to the Maumee River and Buffalo and stopped at ports along Lake Erie and beyond. This meant that business remained steady and profitable for the Captain.

Two years later, the *Helen Strong* was caught in a storm with gale force winds on her return from Buffalo and was forced off shore near Erie, Pennsylvania. The ship was battered by the shoreline and 13 of the 150 passengers lost their lives. The steamer that transported passenger and freight between Monroe and Buffalo was a total loss in the violent storm, together with $9,000 in merchandise intended for the Captain's store at the docks. One of the remarkable traits of Captain Strong was his ability to put adversity behind him and move on. This was recognized and admired by all who knew him. The loss of lives for the first time was a difficult moral dilemma but strong faith and the realization that nature's way is God's way did not keep him from moving on.

Loss of the Helen Strong from "History of Great Lakes" on the internet

Ice Jam at Buffalo. - The elements were terribly destructive to life and property, commencing in the month of March, before the opening of navigation; an ice blockade in Buffalo Harbor, March 14, was without a precedent in lake annals. During this ice jam at Buffalo the Chatauque, Rochester, St. Louis; brigs Empire, Toledo, Maryland, Illinois, Hoosier, Osceola, Globe and Toledo; and schooners Marengo, Woodbridge, Kinnie, Convoy, G.H. McWorter, H. Colvin, Barcelonia, Dayton, Jane Louisa, Rainbow, Superior, Dolphin and Velocity sustained serious injuries. The schooners Avenger, Milan, United States, Emlin, Baltic, Daniel Webster, Vermont, Adair, Huron and Stranger were damaged; steamer Dole sunk.
Thrilling Rescue of the Helen Strong's Passengers. - The loss of the steamer Helen Strong, a boat in her second year, was a most thrilling event. She left Buffalo for Toledo, November 20, about noon, with a large number of passengers and a heavy freight of merchandise, mostly for Erie. When in sight of that port she was struck by a heavy beam sea, which parted her rudder chain. The after cabin was being cut away in order to ship a tiller, when one of her steam pipes burst, and let all her steam escape, but no one was injured by the explosion. Her anchor was dropped, to which she swung for half an hour, when the chain parted, and at about 10 o'clock at night she struck a rocky shore which arose perpendicularly some 30 feet above her hurrican(sic) deck. After striking two or three times she broke in two places, and settling in the sand, remained stationary under the cliff. The first sea that struck her after she settled, carried away the whole weather-side of her cabins, making a clean breach through and through her. Every light had been extinguished by the sea, and the night being very dark, no

one, unassisted, could scale the cliff, and to remain on the wreck seemed quite impossible. At this critical moment it was ascertained that at the first time the boat struck the rock and when she was high upon the wave, one of the wheelsmen and the second engineer, Mr. Munson, with a small cord had made the fearful leap against the rock, and fortunately without knowing anything of the place and not able to see anything for the darkness, they caught the root of a tree that had run far below the surface, by the aid of which they scaled the heights. The wheelsman went immediately in search of help and lights, and the engineer dropped his rope on the deck of the wreck, directing it to be made fast to some light man. It was done, and the man from the top drew up the man from the wreck, and the two drew up the third, and so on until the 60 men, women and children were taken up. Many of the passengers, especially the women, were badly lacerated, by being hauled up so rapidly over those pointed crags. The rope was thrown down and no one seized it, and after frequent and loud calls from the people on the cliff, it was presumed that all were saved who were alive, but on visiting the wreck the next morning several were found alive and taken off. The number of passengers on the boat was not known, and of the dead bodies of those washed off the wreck none were ever found. One woman perished during the night, and was washed overboard. B. Joy, of Sylvania, was seriously injured by the breaking of the rope when being drawn up. His leg and collar bone were broken, but he fell on the deck and was again drawn up and saved. The cliff against which the boat struck was 50 feet high. In the above fearful night the schooner Lexington, Captain Peer, cleared from the port of Cleveland for Port Huron, freighted with 110 barrels of whiskey, 53 tons of coal and two boilers. The schooner foundered in the vicinity of the islands, when portions of the wreck were discovered. The crew, including the captain, consisted of six persons, all of whom found watery graves.

George W. Strong next completed work on the *Baltimore* and launched her in 1846. The *Baltimore* was the largest and finest passenger ship on the lakes and he ran her in partnership with the L. S. & M. B. Railroad. Two years later, the boat was sold and operated out of the port at Sault Ste. Marie Falls and was the first and only steamer running on Lake Superior until the opening of the Sault

Canal.

By 1845, the glory days of LaPlaisance Bay were over and successful businesses relocated to the river where Captain Strong was already well-established. It was only fitting that the last great activity at the Bay involved Captain Strong. When the shipping business at LaPlaisance Bay was abandoned upon the completion of the government canal at the outlet of the River Raisin, Captain Strong purchased and removed the docks. He also moved the largest warehouse over the ice bay to his property on the river during the following winter and rebuilt and used it for many years. That winter, the daring Captain was the most popular man in Monroe and surrounding areas as persons came from far and wide to see the spectacle. Watching the men and horses move the building foot by foot along the ice led the citizens to believe Captain Strong could do just about anything. George W. Strong was now a larger than life pioneer of Old Monroe as LaPlaisance Bay closed its chapter in Monroe history and the River Raisin replaced it as the center of commerce.

The ports at Detroit and Toledo were not standing still during the glory years of the River Raisin. The ports in Detroit and Toledo were improving with freight and passengers, bypassing Monroe. The newer steamers were even going all the way to Chicago. George W. Strong saw that it would be just a matter of time before the future would not be good for the River Raisin. Lake Erie was a blessing to Monroe in the early 1800s but was not so kind in the latter part of the century. Shipping lanes were being developed and the wider and deeper river ports of Toledo and Detroit were becoming more accessible. The boast that Monroe would one day have a greater population than Chicago and Toledo would be short lived.

Strong did not completely envision a time when river access and shipping would not be profitable and Monroe no longer an important port. He could not remember a time when he was not near a stream, river or lake that it did not provide opportunity. As the years passed in Monroe, the qualities of his youth began to change in Strong. These qualities may have been passed down from generations of the Strong family or it may have been unique to George himself.

Adapting and succeeding and the pleasure that accompanies power seemed natural. He was also willing to bear the hardships to fulfill his changing destiny. These passions would pull Captain George W. Strong away from the waters and onto land as he became involved with the railroad.

Captain Strong and the Railroad

Monroe was in its golden years in 1837. Trade at the Bay was increasing and new settlers were arriving every day. Investors knew that work on the River Raisin was only a few short years from being completed but the temptation of prosperity at the Bay was still luring investors.

To write the life history of our esteemed fellow-citizens, Hon. Joseph M. Sterling, would be to give the story of the rise and progress of the principal business and manufacturing interest of the city of Monroe from 1835 to the present time. Up to about 1838, from the peculiar advantages given it by nature, Monroe was the most prominent port on the lakes west of Buffalo and Cleveland, and all classes of merchandise were brought by water in any kind of craft to LaPlaisance Bay, about four miles south of Toll's dock, to which place it was brought through the marsh from the bay in horse boats. (**Wing - *History of Monroe***)

Joseph Sterling was born in New York in 1818. His ancestors first came to the colonies in 1660 and were well-established in the East. Joseph came to Monroe at age 17 and remained in Monroe the rest of his life. He started in the grocery business with J. C. Cole and by 1839, at age 20, had sufficient funds to lease a warehouse at the bay and operate a crude railroad that traveled from the bay to Scott Street in the city. Joseph Sterling, his brother William Sterling and H. Lambert were among the last of the major investors at the Bay.

Business activities began early after the founding of Monroe at LaPlaisance Bay and the first railroad in Monroe was constructed in 1825, with wooden rails and horse drawn cars. The wooden stringers went from the Bay along LaPlaisance Road to Scott Street, stopping at Second Street. This became the River Raisin and Lake Erie Railroad in 1836.

The railroad was later extended along First to Harrison Street. The activity at the Bay included the forming of the LaPlaisance Bay

Harbor Company and its notorious affiliates, The River Raisin and Lake Erie Railroad. Times were good for Monroe in the 1840s. As far east as New York, these same sentiments were shared as the *New York Times* reported:

The village of Monroe, Michigan, one of the rising cities of the West, contains now about 2500 inhabitants. There are about 30 hard goods stores and groceries, 3 hardware stores, 4 clothing stores, 2 grist mills, 4 saw mills, 1 edge tool manufacturer and water power sufficient for 200 homes. Navigation to the village will be implemented in a year or so. Two banks, River Raisin and Bank of Monroe both in a sound condition, being owned by N. Y. capitalists. Also, there are 3 warehouses, 6 steamboats and schooners leaving daily 2000 feet of Warf recently built. A mineral spring has been discovered within a little distance of the village, properties of whose waters being equal to those of Avon. There are between 400 and 500 buildings in the village. Labor is high and mechanics can find good wages.

Monroe began to change as a result of its growth and prosperity. The railroad and better roads were being built. This marked the beginning of a new era for Monroe with many business opportunities that would change the future of the city. In 1842 and 1843, a number of new warehouses were built at the city docks by George Strong and J. M. Sterling. The first shipment of produce was arriving at the port from Adrian by rail. By 1844, Monroe was one of the largest produce markets in the area, receiving wheat from Jackson, Washtenaw and Lenawee counties for shipment to Buffalo. Freight was moving by rail. It represented a new industry that would replace the activities at LaPlaisance Bay and the River Raisin. Inland transportation and infrastructure were necessary for the growing city. Prior to 1845, the forest furnished fuel for the settlers. In 1847, J. M. Sterling brought coal to Monroe by steamer. Over the following years, coal, was to become the primary source of energy. Wagon-making was a less glamorous trade but important and the brickyards were doing well. Flour mills flourished resulting in regular wheat shipments to the port. Farmers began growing grapes and small fruits for the market. By the mid 1800's, gas lighting was developed followed by Western Union and a lumber mill owned by the Sterling brothers. The Monroe area boasted a population of 6,000 in 1840 and was larger than Chicago and Toledo, but changing times lay ahead.

Branches of the Michigan Southern Railroad were among the first railroads to be built and operated in the northwest connecting Monroe to Adrian and Toledo to Adrian in the mid 1830's. The first locomotive appeared in 1835 and was a sight to behold. The final destination of the railroad was planned to reach New Buffalo on Lake Michigan with stops in Hillsdale and Tecumseh. The building of the railroads was marked by success and failures with fortunes made and lost, and delays, delays and delays, but the railroads would eventually reach their final destinations.

The railroad in America had its share of lore and great men. Just as George Strong never expected to be a famous Great Lakes sea captain, neither did he dream that someday the railroad would draw him away from his ships into city life. Strong found that he was spending more time in the city. The city, only one year old, was becoming a magnet for opportunistic men with vision, seeking the fortunes of tomorrow. As early as 1838, one year after the city was formed, George Strong represented the 3rd ward as supervisor. Monroe was growing and the railroad was the focal point for that growth in the late 1830s and early 1840s.

The year 1846 was an important one for Monroe. The state agreed to sell the Southern Railroad built by the state to the Michigan Southern Railroad. Once again, downtown Monroe was the center of activity as the railroad became the main topic of conversation and concern. The railroad was in its early development years and was loosely organized. Everyone wanted a piece of the action, including the State.

There were two concerns for Monroe businessmen. The State was doing a bad job and railroads were not a function of state government. The second was that the Monroe businessmen wanted the control to be in Monroe for the route west to Chicago. They saw, and rightly so, that Toledo and Detroit could be a future threat to Monroe prosperity. Action was necessary.

Captain George Strong, who wanted to complete the cycle from lake to land and then on to Chicago, was among the major organizers to purchase the State-owned Michigan Southern. He was not only a major investor, along with a good number of Monroe businessmen, but encouraged financing from the East. Just as George W. Strong led the way in Lake Erie shipping, he would do the same with the railroad. Strong was well-versed in finance and very adept in managing large sums of money. His skills came from experience and good judgment rather than from any formal education. He had also developed excellent people skills and commanded the highest respect in the community. Together with Charles Noble and T. B. Van Brunt, George Strong would undertake the purchase of the Southern.

The cost of the railroad was $500,000 to be paid on a schedule set by the state. Over half the money was raised by Monroe so that the city would have control of the railroad. Many of the names that were associated with LaPlaisance Bay and the river docks were now older, wiser, more affluent and drawn to the city.

The following list of stockholders is taken from Bulkley's *History of Monroe County*:

Elisha C. Litchfield, New York 1,000shares
W. A. Richmond, Buffalo 500shares
Charles Noble, Monroe 400shares
T. B. Van Brunt, Monroe 250shares
G. W. Strong, Monroe 200shares
Dan'l S. Bacon, Monroe 200shares
Thomas Cole, Monroe 100shares
Morton & Wing, Monroe 100shares
Noble & Sterling, Monroe 100shares
Thomas G. Cole, Monroe 100shares
Morton & Wing, Monroe 100shares
Noble & Sterling, Monroe 100shares
Samuel J. Holley, Monroe 100shares
James Nelson, Monroe 100shares
Fifield & Sterling, Monroe 100shares
Ambrose Beach, Monroe 100shares
N. B. Kidder, Monroe 100shares

Stephan G. Clarke, Monroe *50shares*
Charles Johnson, Monroe *50shares*
Harry Mann, Monroe *50shares*
Geo. Landon, Monroe *50shares*
William Smith, Monroe *50shares*
Isaac Lewis, Monroe *50shares*
William Mitchell, Monroe *50shares*
A. R. Bentley, Monroe *50shares*
David McCormick, Monroe *50shares*
Hiram Stone, Monroe *50shares*
W. M. Stoddiford, Monroe *50shares*
John Miller, Monroe *50shares*
John Burch, Monroe *50shares*
E. G. Morton, Monroe *50shares*
Allen A. Rabineau, Monroe *50shares*
T. E. Wing, Monroe *30shares*
Benjamin Dansard, Monroe *30shares*

It was during this time that the Monroe docks were in their prime and the rail traveled up Front Street and headed west. The prize for the railroad was to be the first to have a route to Chicago. The Southern zig-zaged though Michigan and Ohio but was not the first to arrive at Chicago. The Michigan Central arrived slightly before the locally owned Southern, although it is not historically clear which reached Chicago first.

Steamers were coming from the east on Lake Erie to Toledo, Detroit and Monroe and transferring freight and passengers to rail enroute to Chicago and farther west. There was enough traffic for Monroe to experience its golden years even though Monroe was becoming a pass-through city.

The commissioners of the railroad in 1855 included Hon. David Noble and George W. Strong of Monroe; J. G. Slocum of Trenton; and J. W. Tillman of Detroit. Meetings were held in Detroit. Pressure from stockholders resulted in the commissioners agreeing to open the books to shareholders first in Detroit, then in Toledo and finally in Monroe over a six day period. The Monroe review was in the office of N. R. Haskell & Co. George W. Strong was now embroiled in corporate law and finance with adequate skills and no specialized training. Citizens were concerned that the value of their investment might be compromised in the audit and it was up to Strong to prove otherwise, which he successfully did.

Monroe boomed from 1852 to 1857. New stores were opened, homes were being built and salesmen and promoters stayed in the city and at the hotel at the Lake hoping to cash in on the boom. The Michigan Southern was able to earn millions of dollars over the boom years but could not pay a dividend which was not good for Captain Strong and the shareholders. The ten year period from 1843 to 1853 was the railroad era for George Strong.

First locomotive on the Erie and Kalamazoo Railroad.

The railroad was a turning point in his life. It did something that he thought would never happen; it drew him away from the water. It did not break the bond with the River but set him on a course that once again, he never considered when he was seeking his destiny. The city and the railroad also had an indirect effect on George W. Strong. It drew him into the world of politics. It was this new interest that would change the family man and be most noticeable to Hannah.

Music On The Rails.
Chicago & North Western
RR. Copied from book from
Elsie Little.."The Con-
queror" C/R in 1880

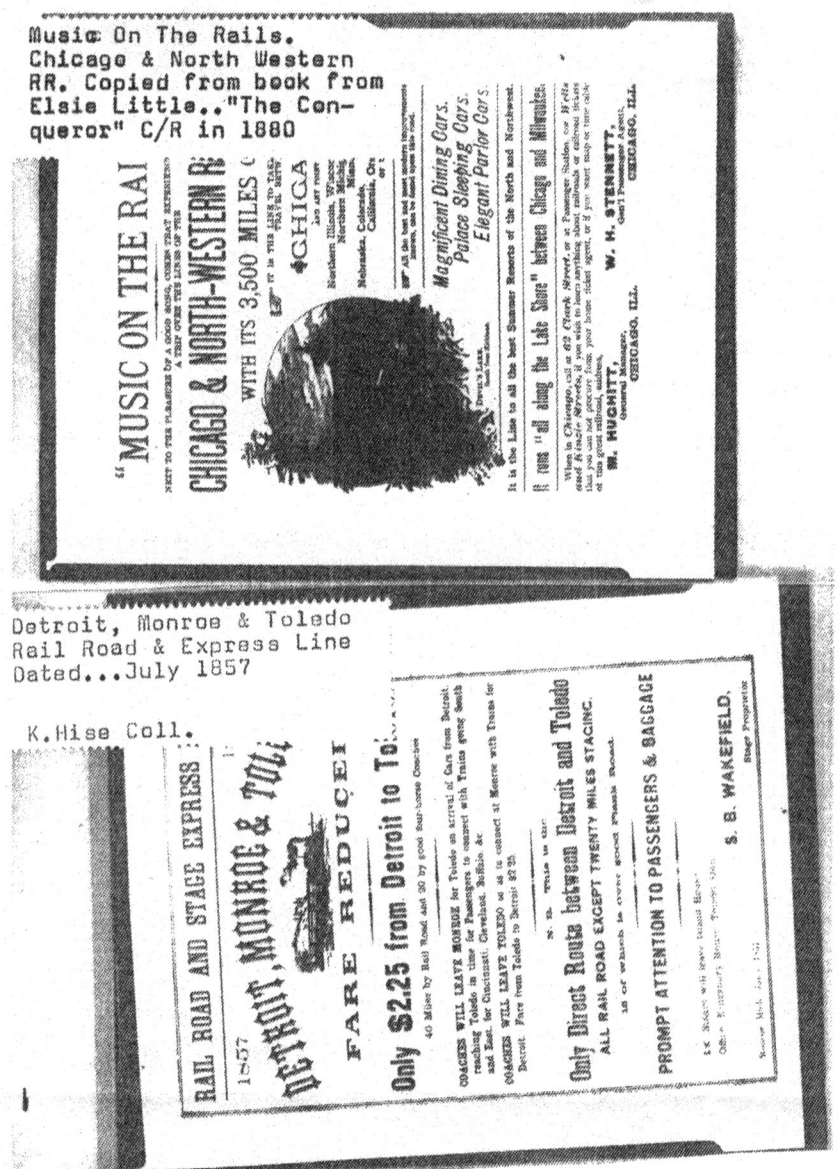

Detroit, Monroe & Toledo
Rail Road & Express Line
Dated...July 1857

K.Hise Coll.

Chapter 6 - **Family Life and Hannah Strong**

As Seen by Hannah Strong

Hannah's perceptions of Frenchtown and her husband, George W. Strong were changing with each letter and brief visit while he was in Frenchtown and she in Norfolk. The changes in her husband, whom she thought she knew so well, made the desire for the family to unite all the stronger. George was no longer the restless searching youth that left Norfolk for the West. As Hannah prepared to leave behind her home of seven years, she was filled with nervous anxiety. Norfolk was a community with good friends and relatives. She would never have been able to survive the time George Strong was in Frenchtown without them. Norfolk was the largest town she had known with nearly 1,000 settlers. She struggled to put the past behind her as she boarded the stagecoach with her six children and began the journey west. She recognized that the future would change reality as she knew it and proceeded to convince herself that it would be for the good.

Tales of Indians and wilderness trails were more fiction than fact by 1835 as the route west had been somewhat tamed and populated. The stagecoach covered nearly 600 miles with stops along the way. The trip for Hannah was not dangerous but trying with the six children. George, 11, and Helen, 9, were a big help with the younger four children. Thomas, 9, and the twins, 7, were hardly able to contain their excitement. All the children except William would remember the adventurous journey to Monroe and share their pioneer experience with friends and family many times over. Hannah saw the experience as only a mother with six children, including a one-year-old baby, could and kept her thoughts to herself.

Many surprises and new experiences awaited Hannah in Frenchtown. She somewhat knew what to expect but reality was different from perception. The village area was a good deal larger than Norfolk and unlike the much smaller settlements of Stockbridge and Chelsea in Vermont. It also seemed that the villagers were more active in a fast-paced community. The downtown was sizeable with stores containing a variety of goods. There was a surprising amount of produce being sold everywhere. There were more farm animals and butchers than in upstate Vermont and Norfolk. The ease in feeding the family was the first comforting thought for Hannah. Not so comforting was what seemed to be the helter-skelter atmosphere of the town. Hannah had heard the term "boom town" with its good and bad and Frenchtown seemed to fit that description.

The months passed, allowing Hannah to become familiar with the settlers in the village. It was a strange mix of people unlike anything she had seen in the East. A good part of the city was French. They seemed to stay on their side of the river or out on the farms and to prefer to be more traditional in their customs. They owned much of the land in the area and specialized in farming.

Hannah found that there were many different things about the French. They did not speak English well and were slow in changing their ways. The French were not well-versed when it came to reading and writing in English but had common sense and a good nature, which made Hannah comfortable since she had limited formal learning herself. Unlike the settlers in the colonies, the French in the village did not consider formal schooling a priority. Strangest of all, they were all Catholic and attended a church that was built long before the Americans arrived. One strange custom, which Hannah did not approve of, was their friendship with Indians. It was indeed a city of two cultures. The new Americans were unlike the settlers Hannah knew back East. Few were involved in the founding of the settlement and most arrived shortly before Hannah. A few months after her arrival, Hannah was no longer a new member of the community. There were new families coming to the Monroe area every week. The one quality the new Americans shared was their enterprising spirit. This spirit contrasted with the French and she could see the American influence slowly change the lifestyle in the city. The continued change to the evolving town, even among the Americans, was just one of many unsettling adjustments facing Hannah Strong.

First Home

The first home for Hannah and the children was on Front Street, where George had been temporarily living while in Monroe. George was somewhat of a squatter when first arriving in Frenchtown in 1832. The city, chartered in 1837 and called Monroe, still had a number of log homes with the transition to frame and brick homes in its early stages. George believed in location rather than status. He could have easily afforded a frame home on Washington Street, which was near the center of town, but that did not serve his purpose. Hannah saw that the converted log home needed improvements for herself and six children and proceeded to provide the comforting touches of a wife and mother. George, who was in no way pretentious when it came to living quarters, was comfortable with the arrangements. He wanted to be in the vicinity of the river where he hoped to one day build his empire - on the gateway to Lake Erie. He sought to be in sight of his fleet and near the men of the lake. He had his priorities, which Hannah did not fully understand. He would spend thousands of dollars on his shipping business but was very modest when it came to personal comfort and status. George Strong was drawn to the River just as his ancestors had been for the past two hundred years. It was in his blood. He was a prisoner of the River which caused Hannah discomfort.

Hannah's expectations were very modest. The harsh Puritan days had passed, giving way to modern dress and newer household amenities. She accepted these changes more for the children than for herself. The mother in her sought safety for the family, food on the table and the companionship of her husband when needed. The modest comfort that George provided in the early years was always more than Hannah expected because she could remember those primitive days in the wilderness. She also knew that it would not be long before George would change along with the city and build a new frame home for the family.

Schooling

Hannah found that there were different approaches to education in the early settlement of Monroe, as was the case in much of the country. The ministers of the reformed churches, Presbyterian, Methodist, Episcopalian, were among the most educated in the community, both in classical learning and social graces. Their denominations preferred to have their churches near the center of the settlement for prestige and convenience. The Catholic priests were equally well-educated in the classics and philosophy but were more protective of tradition and not in favor of public education. The French Catholics did not stress social graces and learning. They were reluctant to expose the children to the ideas of the Reformation. The Americans from New England considered learning one of the cornerstones to building a successful society. One of the highest callings for all early settlers of both religions was to have a son trained in the ministry or priesthood. The common alternative to a formal education was for the son to follow the father in the family trade and daughter to be a wife and mother.

George received the basic New England education which consisted of reading, writing, and arithmetic along with French, philosophy and music. Hannah, unlike George, was not afforded the opportunity of a formal education and was limited in her ability to read or write well. She was not uncomfortable with this because illiteracy was common among pioneer women and men.

Monroe, due to its newness, had not developed a school system prior to the War of 1812. After the war, settlers on the north side of the river, known as Frenchtown, pursued their customs, but education was not one of them. Fishing, hunting, farming and firewood were more important. On the American side, the south of the river, learning began in Sunday Schools and by circuit rider teachers giving lessons. Home-schooling was the most common means of education for the settlers on both sides of the river in the 1820s. It was more successful when the mother, rather than the father, could read and write. Changes began in 1827 when the legislative council authorized townships to hire schoolmasters. This marked the birth of the one-room schoolhouse and one of the first in Monroe was on the corner of Harrison and Fifth Streets. The first private school was conducted by Mrs. Ann Keizer, from 1842 to 1857, and was located at Tremont and Elm Streets. Mrs. Keizer's students were known to learn much more than what was in the school books. Among Mrs. Keizer's more memorable students, she recalled in her later years, were the Strong boys. Other students included Bill and Joe Sterling, Hon. H. A. Conant, Henry Landon, "Gunlock" Bailey and John Bulkley.

The six Strong children experienced schooling in all the changing forms of education with varying levels of interest. The older children, George, Helen and Thomas were schooled in Norfolk, New York, before coming to Monroe and received limited additional education in Monroe. The twins, Alonzo and Thurlow, and young William received their education in Monroe at the same rate that learning in the city improved from 1835 to 1850. Hannah wanted her children to have the opportunity to learn what she did not have. George, on the other hand, was looking forward to the day when the boys would help him in his business ventures. The needs of the family and the desire of the children to learn, varied for each of the Strong children. The children were distinctly different and their choices for the future reflected these differences.

Friendship with Henry and Elvira Smith

Changes observed by Hannah when the family united in Monroe included those with her husband. In his short time in Monroe, George W. Strong gained notoriety and stature. He was very popular in the community and became known as Captain Strong. The citizens were excited about the future of the river canal and Captain Strong, with his ship building, was one of the key persons committed to the future of the River. Hannah expected George to spend most of his time with the family when she moved to Monroe. To her dismay, she felt that she was in competition with the city for his time. Private and public conversations seemed to center around the affairs of Monroe. Hannah, as a result, preferred to remain in her neighborhood near the city docks where the wives shared the same concerns.

Life was becoming complex with new friendships and George's relationship with Captain Smith and Elvira. Captain Smith was the only person George looked up to in the community. Henry Smith, slightly older than George, had a formal West Point education and married a member of a renowned New York family. He had seen much of the known country and fought the Indians in the Black Hawk War. He even told tales of the duel he participated in to defend the honor of a young lady back East. Unlike George he was status conscious and shortly after arriving in Monroe, built the largest home in the city. Captain Smith and Elvira represented the pinnacle in the fledgling city.

North Side of River

Captain Smith retired from the military in 1835, but remained employed by the government and obtained funding from Congress for the River Raisin Canal. His power came from the control of funds for the river project. The river was the common thread that bound Strong and Smith from their first days in Monroe. More important to Captain Strong, Smith was in charge of all Government harbors on Lake Erie. This was also advantageous for the opportunistic Captain

Strong. Both men were driven each for their own reason in their own way.

Henry Smith next ventured into politics in 1838 and 1841, as a Democratic member of the state legislature. The influence of Thomas Jefferson had a profound effect on many of the men of Monroe as they were primarily Jeffersonian Democrats. George Strong was not political and did not share this ambition with Smith but one day he would do something he least expected and be drawn into city politics.

Hannah wondered how two men who were so different in many ways could yet be so compatible. Her more serious concern was with Elvira. George seemed different when in her company. She was one of the most learned women in Monroe and did not live in the shadow of her husband. Her stature was equal to that of Captain Smith. She was Elvira, not the wife of Captain Smith. Hannah, on the other hand, was just the wife of George Strong.

Hannah knew that Elvira aided George during his illness with cholera. She also knew that they developed a friendship during the time she was in Norfolk with the children. Human behavior at times was difficult for Hannah to fully understand. This caused an inner discomfort that would linger for many years. Why did George name his vessel *Elvira Smith* rather than after a member of his own family? He had always said that it was in gratitude for the help of Captain Smith and Elvira when he first arrived in Monroe. This being said, Hannah remained uncomfortable with the friendship and preferred closeness to her children who were nearing adulthood, especially her daughter Helen.

George would often make a special effort to cross the bridge on Anderson Street, then travel east on Water Street passing the Smith home that he helped build. After a visit with Captain Smith, he would travel on to the Macomb Street Bridge and continue home along Front Street. He could not help but notice the difference in status between East Water Street and the homes near the docks on Front Street. Time and again traveling home, he was not swayed by the lifestyle on the north side of the River and remained focused on his personal goals.

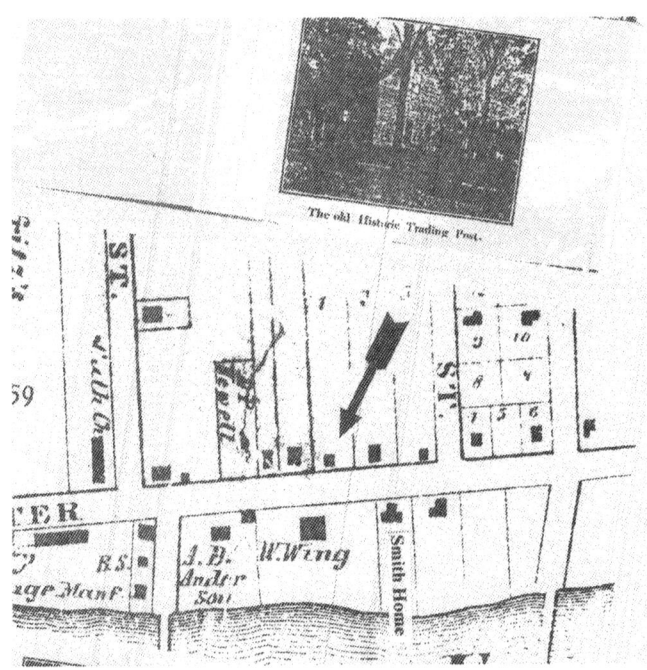

Smith Home and Trading Post

A New Home

A happy moment for the Strong family took place in 1838 when plans for a new home began. George purchased a parcel of property that he had long desired right in the center of the dock area. It was not what Hannah had in mind and it was certainly not her first choice. This was what George wanted because it was good for business. It was to be the site of their first home and Hannah was determined to make the best of this second beginning in Monroe. A frame home was built at the end of Front Street on a new road that was recently built to accommodate the city docks and new River Raisin canal. It was also the location where the railroad would be extended to service the river traffic.

George had acquired a large parcel of land on the south side of the road where he built a large barn east of his home. The only other building to the east of his property was Hurleston's Tavern. Across the road along the river were Cole & Disbrow, Noble & Sterling Warehouse, Fifids & Sterling Warehouse, property where George Strong would later build a marine supply store, the A. A. Rabinean

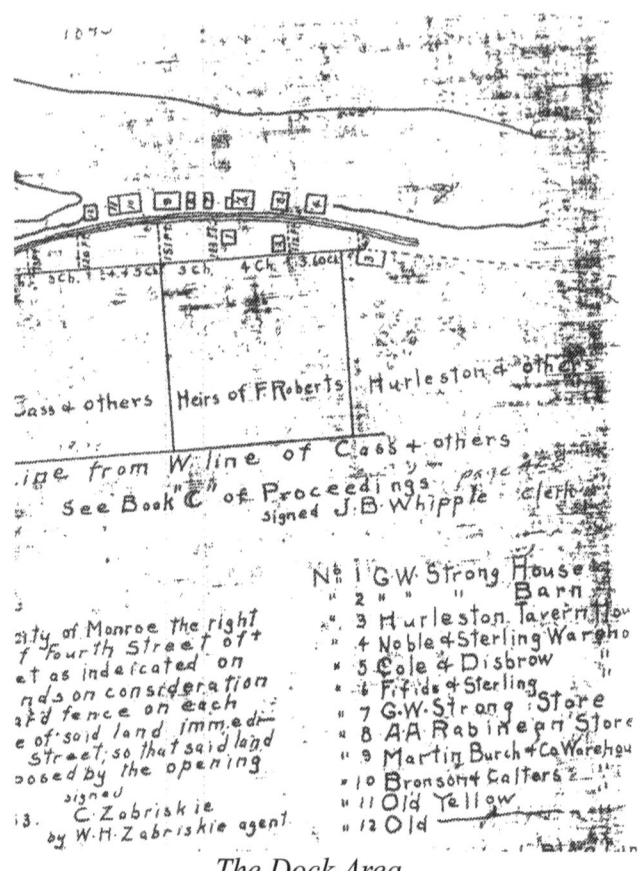

The contents within the map image include various handwritten labels:

The Dock Area

Store, the Martin Burch Warehouse, the Bronson & Calter Warehouse and finally the property belonging to an old seaman known as "Old Yellow". George was correct when he convinced Hannah that the docks would be the fastest growing area in Monroe. Hannah was also correct when she told George it would be far from the most desirable location and it would someday be known as the East End.

1840

Family life and growing up in 1840 were enjoyable times for the Strong family in their new home on the River Raisin near Lake Erie. George was beginning to involve the older boys in the shipping business. The younger children were also involved in contributing to the family prosperity and assuming responsibility as George and

Hannah saw fit.

George A., 16, was the oldest son and had a special relationship with his father. It was the custom for the oldest son to carry on the name of the father and to one day inherit a major portion of his estate. George expected much from his first born and introduced him quickly to the waters of the Lake and the River. His first taste of Lake Erie came as he helped his father at LaPlaisance Bay. Young George was introduced to building ships early and accompanied his father on Lake Erie commercial shipping. As he grew older, he was allowed to assist captains of vessels owned by his father. As a youth, George A. dreamed of the day that he would captain his own vessel. He was a solid young man but could not escape from the shadow of Captain George W. Strong.

Helen was a year younger than George A., and the two shared growing into adulthood together. Both enjoyed water sports in the summer and ice skating in the winter. Skating was best in the city just west of the Monroe Street Bridge. The river waters east of the Isle of Paimos, owned by C. E. Diehl, later known as Sisters Island, were always calmer and froze to a smooth surface. It was a gathering center in winter, one of the best opportunities for young citizens to socialize. Hannah encouraged George A. and Helen to visit the city as often as possible. She wanted them to escape from the isolated docks where Captain Strong was so deeply rooted.

Activities at the Methodist Church in the summer were also a high priority and ones which both parents supported. The families of the most successful businessmen in Monroe attended the services and the Strongs were respected and included in all activities. It was also the gathering where eager mothers entertained the thought of matchmaking.

There was a time for social activities and a time for work. Captain Strong kept the boys focused on their tasks and the family business. Young George would pilot the flat bottom boats in safe waters and assist on short trips between Detroit, Toledo and Canada. The interests of Thomas, 13, and the twins, 11, varied as George attempted to influence them in the most suitable direction for the future. Thomas was least interested in shipping, Alonzo seemed a good worker with modest ambition and Thurlow was more than anxious to climb the ladder to success. William was and always seemed the young one. Captain Strong, at 40 years old, met with the first tragic family death since that of his mother. Mail arrived in Monroe traveling by whatever means were available in early America. It was then held at the post office for pickup. During the winter months persons would

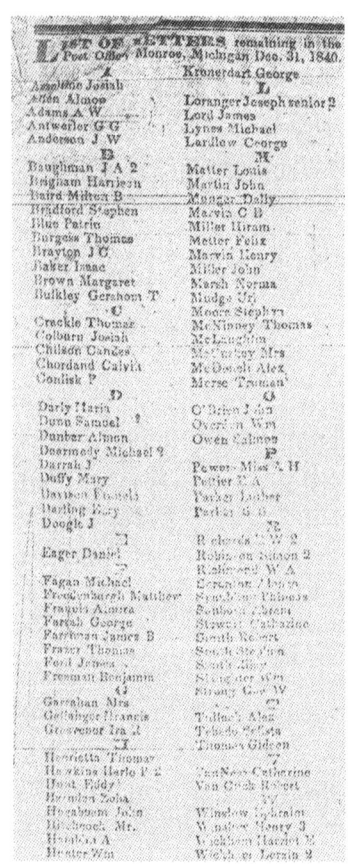

visit town less frequently and the farmers out-county seldom. There was a letter for George Strong at the end of 1840 awaiting pick-up. Following the holidays that year, he rode into town on horseback to discuss the railroad and to get the mail. He picked up a letter from his sister in Vermont at the post office and on that day, the news was not good. She informed him in the letter that his father, John Strong had passed away.

He knew his father was not well of late, but the message of death was far different from news of illness. First guilt, then flashbacks and images, came as fast as his heart rate. He felt sorrow for not being there near the end. He had not seen his father for nearly 15 years. His father was a farmer and that was not the calling George wished to follow. His father died with no meaningful estate which George was determined not to let happen to him. The most disturbing question that always haunted George Strong was why his father left Glastonbury. George favored his mother and saw Glastonbury through her eyes and never accepted the move to Vermont. George had written his father many times and felt that he had proven his worth and brought honor to the Strong name. He accepted the death of his father, confident that his father respected his seventh child, George W. Strong.

1841 Shipping

Lake Erie shipping was a difficult and perilous profession as the Strong family was reminded in 1841. More bad news followed when Captain Strong was informed that the steamboat *Erie* was lost at sea along with his good friend Captain Titus. The ship left Buffalo with 200 passengers bound for Chicago. Four hours out of Buffalo, a fire broke out when turpentine, stored too close to the boiler, exploded. A sheet of flames enveloped the whole boat. Captain Titus raced to the ladies' cabin where 90 to 100 life preservers were stored but the flames kept him from the life vests. He then went to the upper deck battling the flames, violent winds and waves to lower the life boats. The ship was ordered to head toward shore to no avail. Two of the lifeboats were lowered and were immediately swamped by the raging waters. All efforts to save the screaming and panic-stricken passengers failed. Husbands, clinging to their wives and children, kept afloat to no avail until the lake took them. What followed was an agonizing death scene. There was only one female survivor resulting from the Captain handing her an oar to cling onto until help came. The steamboat *Clinton* arrived at the scene the next morning and rescued a small handful of survivors floating around the smoking wreck. Captain Titus was not one of them. The dangers of his chosen line of work were brought home to Captain Strong, who had made a commitment to Lake Erie dating back to 1832.

The event was a turning point for Hannah. It was not uncommon for George, on occasion, to be on the lake for seven days. There was no news of his trip until he arrived home. Every time there was a storm or strong wind, she would fear for his safety. To make matters worse, the older boys were sailors and often on the lake. She began to confront George about his chosen profession.

Captain George W. Strong, on the other hand, had no fear of the sea. He was aware of the danger and knew that great care had to be taken. He also knew that with the risk was the reward. The Lake had been kind to him and his financial gain was notable. He would never admit that he would leave the Lake but he knew one day things would change and it would be time to move on. If he did move on, the railroad seemed the next likely opportunity for profit. That day would be in the future.

1842

With the help of his boys, Captain Strong sought to take advantage of the good times at the Bay and River by building two boats, the *Macomb* and the *Helen Strong* in 1842. Thomas, who was now 15, joined his older brother George, 18, and lent a heavy hand in building the steamers. The twins, Alonzo and Thurlow, who were 12, had their introduction to what would become a family business. Captain Strong included everyone resulting in the boys prospering and becoming established in the community. In time, each of the children would choose his own path, but in their youth, they followed their father.

Captain Strong made the first major commitment to the children in 1844 by making George A., 20, captain of the *Helen Strong* and Thomas, 17, an engineer whose responsibility was to keep the steam engine operating. Thurlow and Alonzo, 15, were too young to captain or engineer, but began to prepare for the future as sailors and engineering assistants.

The family business was prospering. The boys were accepting more responsibility to the dismay of Hannah. Captain Strong, on the other hand, had more time to spend in the city and become involved in the railroad. He was slowly becoming immersed in a new interest. He was also discovering that land in the city was a popular topic of conversation. Fortunes were made in land speculation if bought and sold properly. He also recognized that he was respected and taken into confidence by the local businessmen on opportunities in the city.

By 1844, Hannah was now well-known in the community. She thought the turning point for her was in 1842 when George was a primary contributor to the fundraiser to save the Methodist Church in Monroe. She had been in Monroe for ten years and was very comfortable with herself now. She was accepted by the wives of the English-speaking businessmen as herself and not as the wife of Captain Strong as in the earlier years. She had taken part in many community service activities and aided female friends seeking help. Monroe was now her home.

New homes and land were being developed along Washington, Macomb and Scott Streets. First and Second Streets were also developing on both sides of South Monroe Street. The north side of the river had a few fine homes near the home of Captain Smith but little beyond that. The French did not seem as interested in developing the farmland. Hannah also noticed there was a subtle underlining hostility toward the French. The relationship was friendly on the outside but an air of superiority by the English was hidden on the inside.

Hannah's desire to move away from the docks grew from year to year. She could see that the persons living along the docks were not as refined as those in the city. Her daughter, Helen, was 19 and nearing marrying age. It would be important for her to find a partner away from the docks. She reminded George that the day would come when theirs would be a city life. Little did she know how true this would be.

1845 *Helen Strong* loss

The *Helen Strong* was a special ship for Captain Strong. It was the ship that George A., now 20 years old, would captain. Thomas, 17, was the engineer and Thurlow, 15, was a sailor on the vessel. The anxious Captain was convinced the boys were ready and responsible for shipping between Monroe and Buffalo.

Hannah knew Lake Erie and the dangers of unpredictable weather. There was always the memory of Captain Titus in 1841 and tragedies taking place every year. The boys were on the lake more often and Hannah felt that it was only a matter of time before a tragic event would take place. The mother in her preferred the more structured city life.

The morning of November 20, 1845 in Monroe was wind-blown with storm clouds in the west. In late afternoon, a severe storm battered Monroe, then made its way west. Hannah and Captain Strong knew at once that this would be a problem for the *Helen Strong* that was scheduled to leave Buffalo for Erie, Pennsylvania, at noon. The concerns of Hannah Strong were realized when the family received word that the *Helen Strong* was lost in a storm. George A. and Thurlow were on the vessel when the storm hit the ship at 10 o'clock at night as it neared Erie, Pennsylvania. The storm tossed the ship against a 50 foot cliff and turned it into driftwood. Thirteen persons perished. The ship's cargo included $9,000 worth of merchandise for the Strong store at the docks; it was not insured and was lost. It took two days before the family was informed that the boys survived the wreck and would be returning by stagecoach.

The Strong boys gave their father a detailed account of the disaster on their arrival home. George A. was one of the last to leave the ship as he climbed down a rope and swam to shore battered by the waves. Thurlow left the ship just before George A. and was saved by grabbing the branch of a tree as the battered wreck glanced off the shore. Hannah could only thank God the boys were safe and more than ever prayed that Captain Strong would put the shipping business behind him.

Captain Strong was saddened at the death of the passengers; it was truly a sobering time and began the subconscious process of scoring his mind. Although concerned, he was able to put the incident behind him, pick up the pieces and move on. He had become one of Monroe's most respected citizens and that was not tarnished by the mishap that year. Citizens wondered how he could absorb the financial loss and continue to carry on with business so aggressively. There was no rest for the boys as the Captain launched another ship, the *Baltimore,* in 1846.

The mishap with the *Helen Strong* was another turning point for the Strong family. Few knew LaPlaisance Bay, the River Raisin and Lake Erie as well as the Captain. When two of his sons faced death at such a young age, Strong knew it was time to made adjustments to his business interests. It was time to say farewell to waters of fortune and look inland. Captain Strong began to share Hannah's interest in the lure of the city. This was aided by his being elected Alderman for the Third Ward the same year. City office was not new to Captain Strong as he had previously been elected assessor. Captain Strong had lived in Monroe for fifteen years and was finally was enticed by its advantages.

1847

The Mexican War broke out in 1846. Texas was to become a state and its borders were disputed with Mexico. When the States set the border at the Rio Grande River, Santa Anna declared war on America. Once again, the call to arms went out and Henry Smith replied. Smith, at the age of 48, joined the regular army in spring of 1847 with the rank of Major. Troops gathered in Monroe and Major Smith departed the City on May, 10, 1847, leaving Monroe for the South. Captain Strong volunteered to transport the soldiers on his ship to Toledo where they would continue on the river to Cincinnati. It was the last time the two men would be in each other's company. Each of the men had six children providing a subject for small talk. Then, as men would, they laughed about taming the River Raisin. Both men said farewell and looked forward to the time when they would reunite, each knowing that day would never come.

Major Smith received orders to go to New Orleans, then to Vera Cruz where General Scott's Army had landed. While in Cincinnati, he was paid a visit by Elvira and the children for what they feared would be a final farewell. The military knew that yellow fever was killing as many troops as the enemy. Tired and stressed, two weeks after arriving in Vera Cruz, Major Smith died from the illness.

Hannah was not as fond of Major Smith and Elvira as was George. She did feel sadness that the children were without a father. Hannah could not help but wonder if George would go out of his way to help the widow Elvira knowing that Elvira could well take care of herself. She was somewhat consoled by the fact that both George and the times had changed. A myriad of business ventures was the mistress that captivated the attention of George W. Strong.

Elvira was able to be distracted from her mourning by watching the progress of a new family arriving in Monroe to establish a nursery business. The family located across the road and were converting the Navarre-Anderson Trading Post into a home. The family was German and the nursery man was I. E. Ilgenfritz.

1847 Saw mill

By 1847, George W. Strong had become a man of wealth, power and influence. These are the qualities that change a man. Strong found that just as the rivers and lake and been his passion, the city was now having the same effect. He no longer was interested in spending long nights on an unpredictable lake. Nor did he want to wade in the cold waters to battle nature or change its course. Strong enjoyed building but not the ships that he would no longer sail. Growing power made him want to direct, to order, to advise and to approve.

George W. Strong was financially secure. He could account for every dollar received and spent. Bankers would adhere to his wishes with a handshake. The two investments Strong valued most at this point were shipping and the railroad. American investors were in the middle of a love affair with the railroad. Strong had spent considerable time and capital the previous year with the railroad people. Hannah questioned his commitments to this speculative and very competitive venture. She saw him continued to be pulled even more from the family.

Strong saw an answer for the family in the land. It was not uncommon for land speculators to fall on hard times. Their land would be sold at auction or to anyone interested in purchasing the mortgage. Another perfect parcel of land was available on the river. It was located a little over a mile from the docks and just on the outskirts of the city. The land was east of Winchester Street and the railroad bridge a short mile from the center of town. George convinced the family that the property should be purchased by George A. who was now 23 and that it would be a good home site. The family had made many trips into town along Front Street over the years. They watched the city grow from year to year and knew some day they wanted to be closer to town. Young George needed little convincing to become a major land owner and purchased the parcel of land about a mile from the center of town near the River on Front Street for $200. George A. had prospered helping Captain Strong at LaPlaisance Bay and the docks. The sinking of the *Helen Strong* and its resulting deaths were a factor in the events that unfolded.

Captain Strong had established himself as a city insider and was aware of the progress and problems of its citizens. He learned that Harry V. Mann was having financial problems and wished to dispose of his saw mill and acreage on the river near town exactly where the Strong family hope to relocate. To make the property additionally attractive was the steam saw mill which would be a sure business success for young George. George was convinced that his oldest son would mature with a business that he could call his own, in addition to the family business on the docks. It was then, in 1847, that young George, with his father's blessing, purchased the saw mill and land that went from the River Raisin to Plum Creek for $1,650, a large sum of money at the time for a large plot of land. It was almost half of the East End of Monroe.

George A. was challenged with building the business at the saw mill. A saw mill was successful as long as soft trees were available and they were located near the saw mill. The mill received its power with the help of the River. The demand for lumber was brisk due to the rapid growth of the city and the number of frame homes being built.

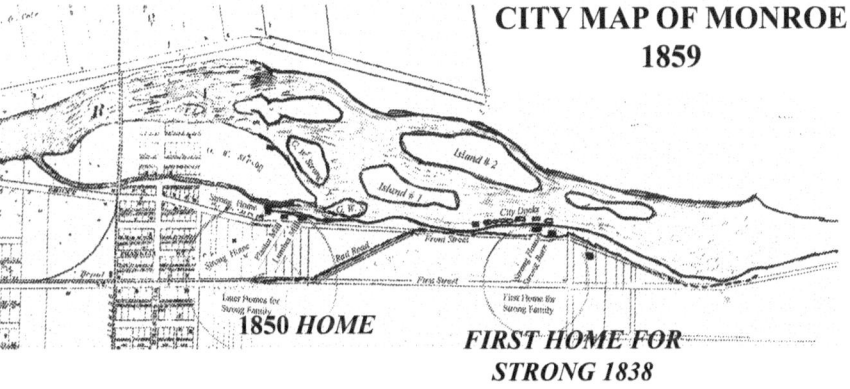

**CITY MAP OF MONROE
1859**

1850 *HOME*

*FIRST HOME FOR
STRONG 1838*

A plaster mill was built on the property next to the saw mill shortly after the lumber business was established and it was successful. It would mark the entry of the Strongs into the construction business. Thomas was 20 years old when the saw mill was purchased. He was assigned to mind the affairs at the docks including the shipping and the store. The twins were 18 and William 13. Alonzo worked as an engineer, maintaining the steam engines first at the docks, then on the railroad and back to the docks. Thurlow had labor and administrative skills and assisted both at the docks and saw mill. George, to a great extent, and Hannah to a lesser degree, were proud of the business venture that would be later known as G. W. Strong and Sons.

New Home in 1850

Hannah was excited by the purchase of land closer to the city. Building a new home was always a part of the dream that both Hannah and Helen had for the future. Construction began in 1849 on Front Street on the west end of Strong Field (Hellenberg Field today), a short walk from the mills. It was a special and busy year since Hannah was also preparing for the wedding of her daughter. The home was completed in 1850 and Hannah was finally able to move away from the docks. Deep down she considered the move a half a loaf since her desire was to live in town on Washington Street. She was on the eastern edge of the city and a mile away from the shipping turmoil of the docks.

Wedding Bells

The children were in their 20s from 1845 to 1855 and had developed friendships with the new settlers in the community. George A. had become acquainted with an Irish Catholic who came to Monroe with his family from Ireland in 1842. His name was Thomas Doyle and he was the same age as George. A friendship developed at the docks where Thomas was a forwarding merchant working for Sterling and Noble and for his father. In his later years, Doyle would become a successful businessman and Mayor of Monroe. The Doyles were a large family and lived in the Second Ward in the area of Scott and

Second Streets. The Doyles were often visited by another Irish family, the Quinns. George and Helen Strong, Thomas Doyle and Crisley Diffenbaugh became close friends as young adults. Helen was close to her parents and was very responsible. She entered adulthood and marriage in a very traditional manner. She enjoyed social activities with young George but looked to her mother for approval on any serious relationship. Helen had been courted by Crisley Diffenbaugh who was three years her senior. The Diffenbaughs were respected members of the community and also attended the Methodist Church. A prominent member of his family was Sir Knight Diffenbough, who was a noted Mason. The Masons were made up of Protestant members of the community and shared business interests and social information. It was considered prestigious to be a member. Helen would marry Crisley in 1849 at the Methodist Church, with George A. Strong and Thomas Doyle as witnesses.

Captain Strong and Hannah could not have been happier when their daughter married a prominent member of the Methodist Church, witnessed by her son George and their best friend Thomas Doyle. Captain Strong was now a father-in-law. The thought of being grandparents had become a reality. However, they would have to wait eight more years for that.

The next marriage in the Strong family would take place in 1853. The circumstance would be different this time. Religion would be a factor in the relationship. Maria was the daughter of Michael and Catherine Quinn who were born in Ireland and moved to Monroe. The Quinns had a son Peter and three daughters. The Quinn children were friends of the Doyles, who were friends of the Strong boys. The Quinns, like the Doyles, were Catholic but this was not a problem for the Strong boys. Maria, one of the Quinn girls, began a relationship with Alonzo that would result in marriage.

Marriages between Catholics and Protestants were discouraged by both parents. The Irish who settled in Monroe did not have the language barrier of the French but did have the same strong religious convictions. In young love, then as now, the partner with the stronger conviction usually had the most influence on the worship of the partnership.

In this case it was Maria, resulting in marriage at St. Mary's Catholic Church in 1853. The marriage was witnessed by Lewis Doyle and Catharine Carrigan, both Catholics.

The Strongs had been in the new land for two hundred years and had adapted to the concept of religious freedom. The marriage of Alonzo and Maria was accepted by George and Hannah begrudgingly and life went on with Alonzo choosing to be more independent in his relationship with the family. Three years later, in 1856, Alonzo was a workman in Van Wormor's Wagon Spoke Factory when one of his hands was injured very seriously by a circular saw. Recovery was slow and the use of his hand was limited. This further removed him from the construction work of his father and brothers.

The purchase by young George of a parcel of land, a short mile from downtown would involve the entire family. George and Hannah built a new home at that location in 1850. Young George also built a smaller home for himself and later sold a parcel to his sister Helen for a home when she married Crisley. Alonzo purchased a lot on Front Street nearby when he married. The entire Strong family was located within a city block of each other. George W. retained his interests on the docks but to a lesser extent as he and the family were becoming city people. Hannah and Helen were most pleased to be closer to the city and a change of scenery. Captain Strong began spending more time in the city. He was an easy choice for Alderman (a councilman) for three years, followed by being elected Mayor in 1855. He knew all the prominent members of both the city and state governments and was also recognized by them.

George W. Strong, now the city man, then pursued two new areas of interest, the railroad and construction in the city. He was a prosperous businessman and finances did not restrict his pursuits. Time spent in the city made him aware of tax sales and persons who were experiencing financial difficulties and wanted to sell property. He purchased five different parcels of land for back taxes in the city. A parcel was purchased from John W. Johnson, a land speculator, on Washington Street in 1858, and an additional parcel on Washington Street in 1860. This was the property where the Strong Hotel would be located. The Strong children, along with Captain Strong, became land speculators and continued to buy, divide and then sell land to each other and others for a profit. However, most of the land purchased would stay in the family during the lifetime of George W. Strong.

Monroe, Mich. City Hall Block, as copied from 1859 Map in Monroe Co. Museum.

City Hall Block

Captain Strong and City Politics

Events were as a tide moving George W. Strong on a course that he had never anticipated. He dipped his toes into city office, then jumped into deeper water with the railroad until finally he was swept into running the City of Monroe from 1852 to 1856. Public office, like the railroad, was not something that Strong ever saw in his future. He was the people's choice and was propelled by the will of the people as he neared the age of 60. He was first elected Third Ward Assessor in 1841 and Alderman in 1846. The demands of public office and the railroad made it necessary to move closer to the city to a home on E. Front east of the Railroad Bridge or Winchester Street.

George W. Strong realized that the railroad in Monroe would some day suffer the same fate as LaPlaisance Bay and the River Canal.

Travel to Chicago would bypass Monroe and emanate from the now larger cities of Detroit and Toledo. His final commitment would be to the city that he had grown to love. He was elected Alderman of the Second Ward and would go on to serve three consecutive terms in that position. The Aldermen not only dealt with city matters with the Mayor, but were also members of the Board of Supervisors for the county. The sessions of the Board of Supervisors were held in the Courthouse in the city. Representatives from all townships were involved: Ash, Bedford, Erie, Exeter, Frenchtown, Ida, LaSalle, London, Milan, Whiteford, Summerfield, Raisinville, and the 1st 2nd and 3rd ward in city. George Strong represented the 2nd Ward and often chaired the meetings because of his status in the city. The population of the county had grown from 9,913 in 1840 to 14,803 in 1850 and 18,076 in 1853. The first year, as Alderman Strong was involved in a committee, he organized matters of support for the poor and the county house. Civic matters of this nature were new to Strong but his skills made it easy for him to meet the challenge. As chairman, in 1853, he was involved in boundary disputes in the county and repairs to the mill below the dam in Dundee.

The year ended with the Board approving repairs to be made to the jail. Strong voted against spending monies on the jail but the motion passed by a 10 - 7 vote. Strong was then appointed to a committee to confer with mill owners along the River Raisin and report their concerns to the Board. Early in 1854, George W. Strong, Chairman, was in charge of a committee on legislation to pass railroad laws and the suit of the citizens against the Southern Railroad. Strong was re-elected Alderman in 1854. The 2nd Ward which Strong represented consisted of 1345 persons: the first Ward 1868; the third Ward, 958. The township of Monroe south of the city included 958 for a city total of 4809 persons. The first meeting of the year was in March, and Strong, once again, was chairman. A controversial matter was rejected at the first meeting. Mr. Shires was denied permission to exhibit his drama of *Uncle Tom's Cabin* in the courthouse. Funds for libraries in the county were approved with Monroe receiving $86.50 for library purposes. Strong voted for the approval to purchase the Lewis farm for use as a county farm by the Committee for the Poor.

The approval passed 9 - 4. The Board followed by approving each town raising its taxes for the purpose of building roads not to exceed the sum of $1,000. Allowance for mileage for board members was approved for the sum of $102.66 with George Strong receiving $4.74.

Strong was elected Chairman of the Board in the fall of 1854. The county house condition was reviewed by the board with a report on the number of sick there. The poor house or county farm was one of the major agenda items of the year.

A special meeting was called in January 1855 to consider the request of township trustees for extra time to pay county taxes. It was then that the Board set the March 1, date for payment rather than the first of the year. Not all motions would go in Chairman Strong's favor. Strong voted "no" to approve extra funds for jail expenses but the motion passed. Mr. Strong introduced the following:

Resolved, That the Sheriff be, and hereby is permitted to suffer the use of the Savior's room for scientific purposes; demanding such compensation, therefore, as he may think proper, and report to this Board, at their next meeting his doings, that the board may be enabled to determine whether to extend, or further permit the use thereof, and that the Sheriff, be responsible for all damages accruing Thereof.

The Ayes were Babcock, Choate, Murphy, Navarre, Shew. The Nays were Brigham, Burch, Chase, Langdon, Strong, Woodward. Motion for passage, lost.

George W. Strong was elected Mayor of Monroe in 1855. The issues that Strong faced as Mayor differed from those of the Board of Supervisors. There was the petition to discharge from jail John and James Murphy and George C. Clark. Isadore Delosh petitioned that the Fourth Street ditch be completed and the Mayor referred the matter to the Street Commission for attention. The Mayor ordered the removal of the fence from Scott Street and the LaPlaisance Turnpike owned by Navarre and Van Wormer. The council approved pay to R. Nims for work done on the bridge embankment on Water Street for the amount of $155.

George W. Strong was consumed by city affairs from 1852 to 1856 and administered affairs of the city as its leader during that time. Following his term as mayor he would no longer seek any public

Looking across the River to the north

office. He was asked many times to serve in a political capacity but declined. It was during this time that he developed contacts of very influential persons and was advised of desirable properties that could be purchased as a tax sale. He was involved in the purchase or sale of 14 different pieces of property in the 1850s. This included the property on Washington Street where he built the Strong Hotel in 1858. City life and involvement in the city would once again change the life of George W. Strong just as life in America was changing. When Strong traveled along East Water Street often referred to as East Elm Street, he no longer thought of the Smith family. He now looked across the River and marveled at the back of the buildings of a growing city.

Chapter 7 - A Time for Building

City in a city

The death of LaPlaisance Bay was followed by the birth and growth of the dock area. Captain George W. Strong was among the first to have a vision for this section of the city. Others left the Bay when the River Canal was opened and joined Strong, who was one of the first to be established there. Morton, Burch & Company; D. Noble & Company; Bronson & Company; Morton & Wing; Morton & Walbridge; Disbrow & Grinnell; Harloston, Haff & Company were instrumental in the development of the river docks. The new commercial area boasted a hotel, five saloons, a bowling alley and enough business and shipping to keep everyone busy.

Development by the docks

THE RIVER DOCKS

Shipping in Monroe came to an end in the late 19th century. The larger ports and newer modes of transportation in a rapidly progressing America began an era of change.

George Strong Jr. was a child of 10 when Hannah and the children joined their father in Monroe in 1834. The River Raisin was a new playland for young George and the children with few neighbors but plenty of activity. The Strong children had the distinction of growing into adulthood, partaking in the development of what could be called Monroe's first subdivisions. Young George A. Strong could see the changes in Front Street, the docks and the city, day by day, month by month and year by year. The docks, the bars, a bowling alley and the sailors became part of the young man's life as he grew into adulthood.

There were advantages to having a father who operated one of the most successful shipping companies at the docks. The oldest son, George A., knew that someday he would manage the family business. Somewhat assured of success in the future, his self confidence continued to grow and like his father, he was not fearful of taking risks.

The Father kept the boys involved in his business but especially young George, as was the custom for the first born. George W. Strong saw in his son qualities that differed from his own. He was private while the son was outgoing. He paid attention to detail; his son was more helter-skelter. He gave much thought before venturing into a new business; young George went charging into the unknown. George W. Strong was shaken by events; George A. Strong moved on more quickly as was the case with the *Helen Strong*. Despite all these differences, George Strong and son grew closer as the young man became an adult.

Hannah's relationship with her oldest son differed from that of her husband. Hannah considered the docks and its patrons as a negative influence on the children. She preferred that George A. be a patron of the city and downtown. Hannah did not approve of the ladies who frequented the dock area. Young George realized this, and unlike his brothers and sister, was not eager to marry. George A. Strong did not give up his free spirit as he grew older, resulting in numerous friends and a trademark as one of the most eligible young men in the city. George A. Strong continued to live in the home of his mother and father, although he came and went as he pleased. Hannah, more than her husband, feared that one day his behavior would cause her grief as time passed and talk of a Civil War escalated.

George W. Strong paid the boys well for their services and insisted that they save for the future. He was more conservative than the boys almost to a fault and did not see the importance of insuring his investments as was the case with the *Helen Strong,* where he suffered a financial loss. Business was so good for the Strongs, that despite an occasional mishap, they remained financially secure.

Time and events were leading up to the next major venture for George W. Strong, the family, and the building of the Strong Hotel. The year was 1847 and at the age of 23, George A. Strong began to assert his independence by purchasing a saw mill located on a large parcel of land on Front Street near the family home. The proud and hopeful father bypassed the investment for himself, encouraging his son in the new business venture. It was the right time in Monroe for that type of a business and George A. prospered from the time of the purchase. The Strong name was enough to secure many contracts for lumber. The contractors involved in home building were friends of George W. Strong, who was Alderman and Mayor ,which made sales of lumber immediately successful. Political ties enabled young George to get the contract for the lumber to build city sidewalks. Financial success resulted in expansion into a plaster and gypsum mill for the builders. During the 1850s, George A. and home builders in Monroe were in their glory years.

Building was not new for the Strong family. They had built ships, warehouses and homes in the past. With the purchase of the lumber mill, they began building homes in the city, which was not difficult with the ownership of a lumber and plaster mill. In order to be a successful builder George W. realized that land ownership was essential. Political ties served a useful purpose as he became aware of one select purchase after another. Acquisition and speculation in land began in earnest in 1854 for the Strongs.

Liber 43, page 293, dated 18 January 1854, recorded 26 January 1854, Joseph C. Cole and wife sold to Thurlow Strong, a parcel of land in the city for $1.00, known and described as a lot on the Duval or Hatch farm. 125 feet deep to the River Raisin from Front Street and 96 feet wide.

Liber 44, page 442, dated 1 June 1854, recorded 22 September 1854, George A. Strong, sold to Helen Diffenbaugh, for $100.00 a parcel of land 100 feet square in the Northwest corner of land bought and recorded 18 February 1850, in Liber QQ, page 212.

Liber 44, page 479, dated 25 September 1854, Recorded 30 September 1854, George A. Strong sold to Hannah Strong, a parcel of land in the 2nd ward of the city for $200.00. Starting at a stake on the North side of Front Street, 150 feet Westerly from the East line of the Johnson farm, and running Westerly on the South side of said Front Street. 200 feet to a stake, running Northerly on a parallel line with the line of said Johnson farm, to the South branch of said river to a stake, running Southwardly in a parallel line with the East line of said farm to stake place of beginning, containing about 2 acres of land more or less.

Liber 45, page 320, dated 3 February 1855, recorded 14 March 1855, Witney Jones, Auditor General State of Michigan, sold to **George W. Strong**, for delinquent taxes not paid for year 1851. Purchased on 3 October 1853, for $24.80, twenty-four dollars and eighty cents. The undivided half of ten acres of land bounded North by River Raisin, East by Suzor farm, South by branch of River Raisin, West by Menard Farm (so called) or Stuart plot. Also lots No. Two Hundred, Wadsworth and Navarre lot all in the city of Monroe

Liber 45, page 321, dated 3 February 1855, recorded 14 march 1855, Witney Jones, Auditor General State of Michigan, sold to **George W. Strong**, for delinquent taxes not paid for years 1851 and 1852. Purchased on 2 October 1854, for $11.93, a parcel of land situated in the city, bounded North by River Raisin, East by Cauchois estate, South by Front Street and West by Cauchois estate, containing Three Acres and Fifty Hundredths of an acre more or less.

Liber 45, page 322, dated 3 February 1855, recorded 14 March 1855, Witney Jones, Auditor General State of Michigan, sold to **George W. Strong**, for delinquent taxes not paid for years 1850, 1851 and 1852. Purchased on 2 October, for $22.80, a parcel of land 52 acres in size, bounded North by the city line, East by march, South by Plum Creek and West by **Strong.**

Bank of the River Raisin Building

America gained its independence in 1776. It would take years and the efforts of Alexander Hamilton to establish a standard currency and a banking system for the new nation. Until regulations were put in place, banking was the business of merchants and speculators in the era of the Wild Cat Banks. The opening of the Erie Canal in 1826 had a direct effect on Monroe and Detroit. Transportation from the East became easier, bringing travelers, trade, speculators, boom times and the Wild Cat Bank to Southeastern Michigan. As banking became more regulated, the first legitimate bank established in Monroe was the Bank of the River Raisin established around 1834. It was the first effort at a major and permanent bank operating out of its own building. The bank was located on Washington Street with its imposing Corinthian columns across its 27 foot front.

The bank was located on the northwest corner of the Public Park

Odd Fellow Hall

and Washington Street. The Odd Fellows Hall was on the north side of the building. Banking continued in this building until 1844 when it issued its last notes. The president was Austin E. Wing.

The vacant building did not go unnoticed by George W. Strong. It would play a role in the new direction that he and his family next followed. Strong had become a man of many diverse interests. His sons were also branching out into new business ventures. The hub of activity was no longer at the docks. Strong knew that future opportunities would be available only through close associations with the city.

It took a few short years for Austin E. Wing to complete the process of dissolving the Bank of the River Raisin. The vacant building was a landmark in Monroe and vacant when George W. Strong was ready to relocate his business office to center of the city. He secured a rental agreement with the owner and the building became the downtown office for George W. Strong & Sons. It was not until all banking passed out of existence in the building that he was joined by old friends Stephan G. Clarke and Dr. William M. Smith. The building also became the private banking office of Smith and Clarke, a firm organized in 1858.

The new office downtown location was marked by continued speculation in the purchase of land by the Strongs.

Liber 45, page 322 & 323 dated 3 February 1855, recorded 14 March 1855, Witney Jones Auditor General of Michigan, sold to **George W. Strong**, for delinquent taxes for 1852. Purchased 2 October 1854, lot number two hundred Wadsworth and Navarre plat in city of Monroe, for the sum of $3.25. No size shown.

Liber 45, page 323, dated 3 February 1855, recorded 14 March 1855, Witney Jones Auditor General State of Michigan, sold to **George W. Strong**, for delinquent taxes for 1852. Purchased 3 October 1853, undivided half of Ten Acres of land in the city of Monroe, bounded North by River Raisin, East by Suzor farm, South by branch of River Raisin, West by Menard farm (so called), or Stuart plan, for the sum of $14.10.

Liber 45, page 533, dated 26 March 1855, recorded 21 May 1855, George W. Strong , sold to **William V. Strong**, a parcel of land in the 2nd ward of the city for $100.00. The lot bounded North by River Raisin. East by Cauchois estate, South by Front Street, and West by Cauchois estate containing Three and Fifty Hundreds acres more of less.

Liber 52, page 247, dated 26 march 1855, recorded 16 June 1859, **George W. Strong**, sold to Thomas T. Strong, a parcel of land in the 2nd ward of the city of Monroe, for $150.00. 10 acres of land bounded North by the River Raisin, East by the Suzor farm so called, South by branch of River Raisin, West by Menard farm so called, in the Stewart plot.

Liber 49, page 625, dated 7 April 1855, recorded January 1858, Charles G. Johnson and wife sold to **Thomas T. Strong**, a parcel of land, part of the Suzore farm so called which lies between Front Street and First Street in the city of Monroe. Bounded on the East by the Duval or Hatch Farm and the West By the Joseph Roberts farm. Containing 5 acres more of less, for $900.00.

Liber 49, page 224, dated 28 January 1856, recorded 27 July, Thomas G. Cole and wife sold to **Alonzo Strong**, a parcel of land, known as lot number 34 on the Stewart plot, so called for $40.00. No size shown.

Liber 54, page 70, dated 16 January 1860, recorded 16 January 1860, George W. Strong sold to **Chrisley Deffenbaugh**, **Thurlow Strong** and **William Strong**, the equal undivided half of a parcel of land situated in the city for $600.00. Bounded Eastwardly by Washington Street, Southerly by lot now belonging to **Chrisley Diffenbaugh** and Hannah Strong, and lot of Allen A. Robinson, held for use of Trinity Church, West by said church lot, lot of Robinson and alley, North by lot of Stephan B. Wakefield. The lot being 50 feet in width on Washington street, and same lot recorded in Liber 52, page 59.

George Strong and the Union School in 1858

George W. Strong, Steamboat Properties on Front Street, was the way Strong was described in the city directory in 1856. His son, George A., Saw @ Gypsum Mill on Front Street was the next entry. Strong was nearing 60 and thought that he was nearing his later years. He had put a demanding period of politics behind him, thinking it was time to slow down. The boys were doing well and assisting them seemed to be a good choice for his twilight years. His desires were short-lived. Strong had a long future and many more historic years yet to live before his final chapter would be written. He had established himself in a city that could not exclude him from its progress. He could not turn his back on the self that kept saying more, bigger and better. As in times past, he was to be drawn again to change and progress. George W. Strong and Sons began the process of seeking the next attractive business opportunity in the City of Monroe, but first there was the Union School.

Captain George W. Strong would play a role in the growth and development of education in early Monroe by being one of the main contractors to build the Union School in 1858. It is interesting to note that Congress, in 1787, ordained that 168 acres in every township be reserved for education. The Monroe district could not determine where this much land should be located. Land for the University of Michigan was finally allocated in Toledo, then part of Michigan. The University of Michigan was later moved to allocated land in Ann Arbor. The businessmen and entrepreneurs chided the farmers, part in jest and part in sincerity, that if they were not so greedy with their land the University would be in Monroe. Provisions were made for education in a disorganized-organized manner by the Americans in Monroe from 1820 to 1858. First there were home schools and Sunday schools. This was followed by a number of private schools taught in the basement of churches and in homes. The Rose Cottage Home School and Boyd School were two of the most famous. The school system was in need of organization, not only in Monroe, but throughout America. The early solution was to build what were called Union Schools. They would be a consolidation of all the smaller schools into one larger school. This concept was opposed in Monroe by the French Catholics, who not only did not want to pay for such a program, but also did not want their children exposed to the modern influence of the Reformation and Protestantism. In 1846, the first parochial school system was initiated by three Sisters, Servants of the Immaculate Heart of Mary, who came to Monroe at the request of Fr. Louis Gillet from St. Mary's. Although it was called St. Mary's Academy, it was an elementary school for children of St. Mary's Parish. The first parochial school opened with 44 students, four of them boarders. A second parochial school was founded about the same time at St. Michael's Parish. One of the most important contributions to the community was that besides the three Rs, English was taught to the French and German children. By 1858, the attitude toward education, thanks to the efforts of the parochial schools to promote a common language, began to change and the community was in agreement to build a Union School after an election.

A vote approving the public school for grades 8 through 12 was passed in June 1858 and a celebration took place as the cornerstone was laid. The ceremonies included a number of speakers, bands, a parade, and active participation by the Masons. Among the speakers was John Strong, a rising political figure who felt strongly about education.

John Strong of Rockwood

George W. Strong admired the young politician and was drawn by the family name. He was impressed with the demeanor and remarks of the speaker. John Strong contended,

"The community schools should have the first consideration all the time. The strength of the government comes from the masses and it is in community schools that a very large majority of the masses receive all their book education. Americans must strive to give the masses the very best education we can before we turn our energies to higher education. College education is very important but few are able to attain it while many have to quit school without a complete education due to the hardships of the time. The Monroe school should be the model for the county".

The cornerstone event began a long friendship between the two men. They had the same work ethic, conservative lifestyle and distant ancestors in England. John Strong was born in Detroit on Holden Avenue, a short distance from Grand River Avenue. His father emigrated from England to Canada and settled in Detroit on 500 acres of government land. His nearest boyhood neighbor was a mile and a half away. The men enjoyed sharing tales of hardship as youths in America. John Strong remembered the times when he was eight years old and the family ran out of coal in the dead of winter. He had to trek a mile and a half to the neighbors to get coal, and then back with the heavy load. He chuckled that matches were not available in those days and everyone used steel and flint. School was a two and a half miles walk from home to the west. John Strong, born in 1830, remembered when there was not a foot of iron pipe and an old Frenchman sold the city bored out logs for water pipes. Grand River Road was not open and the way to town was through Springwell Road to where Fort Wayne stood.

George Strong wondered why John was a Democrat. The answer

was common to most at the time. The first reason was that a Democrat, Thomas Jefferson, drafted the Constitution and Andrew Jackson was able to sustain it in civil and military life with his victory in the War of 1812. "No better constitution was ever framed by men," John often said. The first elected office John Strong held was that of a member of the legislature in 1869. He held many political offices over the years, ascending to lieutenant governor in 1890. He moved to South Rockwood near Monroe in 1863 and built a store and a mill. He owned a 500 acre farm which was very profitable. He became known as the other Strong family in Monroe County and George W. Strong took pride in the fact that their ancestors could be traced back to the ancestors of Elder John Strong.

Construction of the School

By 1858 the businesses at the docks were of secondary interest to George W. Strong. The man who was first at the docks was one of the last of Monroe's pioneer fathers to make a major commitment to downtown Monroe. The commitment started with the Union School.

THE UNION SCHOOL

Everything was in place for another bold move in the life of George W. Strong. The success of the lumber and plaster business led to a natural progression into large scale construction. The man who built ships, warehouses, and homes and even moved a large building across the ice had no fear of being a major contractor in building the Union School.

The school was to be an impressive three-story structure and Captain George Strong with his experience in building received a major contract and was one of the primary builders of the school. Work on the school kept George and his sons busy until April of 1859, when work was completed. The saw mill and plaster mill on the river were yielding the results that both George W. Strong and his oldest son had anticipated. The family was spending most of its time in the city away from the docks. The school did two things which George W. never, once again, dreamed would happen. It cemented his departure from a style of life that he had known for 58 years of his life and introduced him to the process of constructing a major commercial building. It also served the purpose of introducing the family to another new major project. It prepared them for the next milestone in their lives, the building of the Strong Hotel.

The building of the Strong Hotel

The Strong boys were in their late 20s and had prospered in the various family businesses. George A. was the first to buy land near the city. Thurlow made the next purchase in 1854 and worked for his father as needed and had a worth of $600. Thomas worked as an engineer on the steamships when acquiring acreage along the river. Alonzo purchased his property in 1856 and had a net worth of $1,000. Alonzo was not closely associated with the affairs of the family and had a variety of different employers. Helen was the most stable and the closest to her parents. Her husband, Christian (Crisley), was an engineer who had a net worth of $4,500.

Day-to-day activities did not prevent George W. Strong from looking to the future. The mid 1850s marked the beginning of a radical change in his plans for the future. He began to consider the long term financial security of his family. More importantly, he became intrigued by the vacant property next to the Odd Fellows Hall. The plans for a downtown hotel began to grow with each passing day. The vacant property was purchased by John Johnston and others during the time when Monroe was prime real estate for speculators. Land values had since decreased and the owners were either up in years or deceased. The estates' sales were an opportunity for local developers to reclaim their city.

The problems of the city were much different from those of maritime shipping. The city was facing a change with the railroad. Its citizens were able to board the train and shop or visit in Detroit and Toledo. The larger cities were luring the citizens with advertisements promoting discount prices. Usually the advertised items were not available but this did not stop the shopping sprees. The Monroe merchants continued to improve the downtown but could not agree on the best solution. An often mentioned option was a downtown hotel near the train station, which was located on the corner of Monroe and First Streets.

Vacant property owned by John W. Johnston and Adelgunda Murzscmitt

Future Site of Hotel

George W. Strong was aware of these concerns and the idea of a hotel was becoming a reality. Strong first heard that the Washington Street property was going to be for sale in 1857. His negotiating skills resulted in finalizing the purchase of the property he had been eyeing for years. It seemed a replay of his purchases on the River. The strategy of being patient and being prepared always had its reward in the end.

Strong was increasingly aware of land that speculators were selling in default through tax sales. With the boys, except for young William, George W. began accumulating land. Thanks to a friendship with the Auditor General of the State of Michigan, he purchased a five acre parcel for $24.80, a three acre parcel for $11.93, a fifty two acre parcel for $22.80, a lot for $3.25 and ten acres for $14.10. This was a good portion of the land on the east side of Monroe, south of the river. The purchase that would change his life for the next twenty years took place in 1859. Hannah had always dreamed of a home in the city on Washington Street. George, nearing 60, and still an ambitious man would fulfill her dream, but with an opportunity for himself. George W. Strong satisfied his passions and purchased the lot on the west side of Washington Street next to where the old bank of the River Raisin once stood between Front and First Streets for $125. One month later, he purchased another lot adjacent to the first for $1,000. The first property was put in the name of Hannah and the second in the name of George W. and Thomas. George A. was established with the mills; now Thomas would be established as a partner in the Hotel. A commitment to the future was now cast in stone.

Purchase of Hotel Property

Liber 50, page 78, dated 8 February 1858, recorded 9 February 1858, John W. Johnston and wife Sarah from Detroit, Michigan, sold to **Hannah Strong**, a parcel of land situated in the city of Monroe, for $125.00. The following describes the parcel of land, part of lot number 41, old village plat, East of Monroe Street, bounded on the North by lot belonging to heirs of Francis D. Wurzschmitt, on the South by the lot on which is situated the old bank of the River Raisin, in the West by lot belonging to the Episcopal Church, being part of said lot. Fronting on the West side of Washington Street.
Site of Strong Hotel

Liber 52, page 59, dated 26 March 1859, recorded 30 March 1859, Adelgunda Murzschmitt, sold to **George W**. and **Thomas Strong**, a parcel of land situated in the city of Monroe, for $1,000.00. Bounded Easterly by Washington Street, Southwardly by lot now belonging to **C. Diffenbaugh** and **Hannah Strong**, and lot of Allen A. Robinson, for the use and benefit of Trinity Church, West by said church lot, and lot of Robinson and an alley, North by lot of Stephen B. Wakefield. The lot herby conveyed being Fifty feet in front of Washington Street.

(Site of Strong Hotel)

Liber 54, page 16, dated 6 December 1859, recorded 24 December 1859, **George W. Strong** and wife **Hannah** and **Thomas T. Strong,** sold to Charles Taylor, a parcel of land situated in the city for $55.00. 7 feet 6 inches of land equal width from front to rear, off the West side of the parcel of land. Bounded North by the River Raisin, East by the warehouse and lot owned by Cole and Distow, South by Front Street, West by the warehouse and lot now owned by said Charles Taylor.

The property was in the heart of downtown Monroe and on Washington Street. The city had grown from 2,813 in 1850 to 3,892 in 1860. The improved railroad connected Monroe, Detroit and Toledo, bringing new settlers every day. A good idea, no matter where it originates, was one to pursue for Strong. The downtown hotel was a concept that picked up momentum in the mind of Strong. When it was time to build, Strong knew exactly how it should be done. Strong was somewhat of an artist and had sketched ideas for the building many times. He would use the existing Odd Fellows Hall as part of the hotel and build to the north using the same design. When completed, the existing and new structures would resemble a new building modern in every way.

The Union School was not quite complete when George W. Strong finalized preparations and began construction of the hotel. Captain Strong had accumulated a net worth of $11,000 which was considered prosperous for those times. He had the asset of five hard working boys to assist him. From the only open piece of prime property in the city, rose the Strong Hotel. It was the largest building in the city and one of the finest hotels in the state. The Hotel was conveniently located one block from the train station. It was within walking distance to all the homes in the city. The hotel covered all

New Strong hotel

of the property since little space was needed for parking horse and carriages. A new era was to begin for downtown Monroe. The only flaw that Strong could see was that the paint on the new section was slightly darker that that of the Odd Fellows building.

1860 - 1861

For years, it had been Captain Strong, the successful steam boat captain. He would, at the age of 60, assume a new identity, George W. Strong - Proprietor of the Strong Hotel.

The massive undertaking lured business opportunities away from the docks and a new involvement for the children. George A. Strong, the oldest son, was made the official proprietor of the Strong Hotel, assisting his father. William and Thurlow were engineers, keeping the hotel operational. Alonzo once again elected to carve his own path and was a laborer for the railroad and living on Front Street. Helen joined her father at the hotel.

The Strong Hotel was the cornerstone of downtown Monroe and was in the early stages of becoming the focal point of Southeastern Michigan. Strong joined many familiar names that moved from the docks and railroad to the downtown area.

LOOMIS & TALBOTT'S

MONROE

City Directory,

AND

BUSINESS MIRROR,

FOR 1860-61.

REVISED AND PUBLISHED ANNUALLY.

PRICE $1.00.

COMPILED BY

GEORGE W. HAWES, DETROIT.

1860.

The Commercial, Thursday, August 11, 1859

The Improvements in Monroe County cont.

On the corner where the Exchange once stood is to be
J. M. STERLING'S BLOCK
It is forty feet on Washington Street and twenty feet on Front Street, and runs back between Wakefield's and Godfroy's Stores. The corner is to be occupied as an Exchange and Banking Office by Dansard and La Fountain. The remaining portion is to be fitted for a store. The whole is to be four stories in height, the first twelve, the second eleven, and the last two ten feet in the clear. On Front Street just east of Sterling's block is to be

THEODORE GODFROY'S STORE
This is to be twenty by forty-six feet and to be three stories in height.

On the West side of Washington Street just south of the old Post Office building C. G. Johnson has erected a building for
WING AND JOHNSON'S BANKING OFFICE
This is twenty feet wide and forty feet deep, two stories in height, the first thirteen and the second twelve feet in the clear. The front is one of the finest in the city, and is adorned with an elaborate and heavy stone cornice. Mr. Johnson intends next year to build another building similar in style adjoining this, on the site of the Old Post Office.

On Front Street just west of the Hardware store of W. H. Boyd is being erected
E. G. MORTON'S STORE
This is twenty feet in width, and seventy feet deep, three stories high, the first eleven, the second ten and the last eleven feet in the clear. The front is of pressed brick, with iron pillars, window sills and caps, which produce a fine effect, and make it one of the most imposing fronts in the city. It is to be well finished and to be occupied as an auction store by Oscar Stoddard, Esq.

On the east side of Monroe Street stands
MARTIN & KASSELMAN'S BLOCK
Containing two stores, each twenty feet wide and fifty feet deep, and three stories high, with a handsome plain brick front and stone window sills and caps. These stores are each to be occupied by Martin and Kasselman, respectively as a boot and shoe and a clothing store.

On the west side of Monroe Street, on the corner of First and Monroe Street is
DANIEL NOBLE'S STORE
Twenty four feet wide and sixty one feet deep, three stories high, the first eleven and the other two ten deet in the clear. There is to be a still further projection in the rear of the size of eleven by twenty feet of the same height of the main building. This store is to be occupied by Mr. Noble as a Grocery and Provision Store.

On First Street, on the sire of the old Hall of the Sons of Temperance, which was burnt a few months since, stands
HUBBLE'S BLOCK
A portion of which is to be used as stores, or offices, and the rest as a residence.

JUDGE BACON'S STORE

This store now in process or erection stands on Washington Street next north of the City Hall is to be twenty three feet wide and eighty feet deep and three stories in height, each story to be twelve feet in the clear.

T. G. COLE'S STORE

Is to be twenty feet wide and eighty feet deep and three stories high, each story to be twelve feet.

JAMES ARMITAGE'S STORE

Is to be the same size throughout of T. G. Cole's, as also is

S. B. WAKEFIELD'S STORE

These four stories stand together and are to form one block, fronting eighty four feet on the east side of Washington Street. The first story is to be faced throughout with stone, with stone pillars and caps. The remaining stories are to be of pressed brick, with stone window sills and caps. The whole is to be elaborately (sic) and tastefully finished, and will make four stories nor to be exceeded for beauty and convenience in this region of the state.

On the corner where the Exchange once stood is to be

J. M. STERLING'S BLOCK

It is forty feet on Washington street and twenty feet on Front Street, and runs back between Wakefield's and Godfroy's Stores. The corner is to be occupied as an Exchange and Banking Office by Dansard and LaFountain. The remaining portion is to be fitted for a store. The whole is to be four stories in height, the first twelve, the second eleven, and the last two ten feet in the clear. On Front Street, just east of Sterling's block is to be

THEODORE GODFROY'S STORE

This is to be twenty by forty-six feet and to be three stories in height.

On the West side of Washington Street just south of the old Post Office building C. GF. Johnson has erected a building for

WING and JOHNSON'S BANKING OFFICE

This is twenty feet wide and forty feet deep, two stories in height, the first thirteen and the second twelve feet in the clear. The front is one of the finest in the city, and is adorned with an elaborate and heavy stone cornice. Mr. Johnson intends next year to build another building similar in style adjoining this, on the site of the Old Post Office.

On Front Street just west of the Hardware store of W. H. Boyd is being erected

E. G. MORTON'S STORE

This is twenty feet in width and seventy feet deep, three stories high, the first eleven, the second ten and the last eleven feet in the clear. The front is of pressed brick, with iron pillars, window sills and caps, which produce a fine effect, and make it one of the most imposing fronts in the city. It is to be well finished and to be occupied as an auction store by Oscar Stoddard, Esq.

On the east side of Monroe Street stands

135

STRONG'S HOTEL

George W. Strong was once again surrounded by the business men and pioneers he had known since 1830. He was able to provide his family with a legacy that would last for generations, the Strong Hotel. He thought he was in his waning years and his children comfortably settled into adulthood. He would be wrong on both assumptions.

Chapter 8 - Tragedy

Troubling Times

Fear of the Indians lurked in Hannah's imagination as a child. She was a victim of the tales of the old days told to her by her elders. That fear remained with her as a young mother while traveling through Vermont and later upper New York to Norfolk. The Indians killing the white men and the white men in turn killing the Indians was difficult to accept. Hannah thought the killing had come to an end, only to see the killing continue as the English replaced the Indians as the enemy. Her fear of wars faded as the family became engrossed in the activities in Frenchtown. Monroe provided the safety she long desired as she reared her children into adulthood. The management of the new hotel was filled with day to day problems and new challenges that kept the family involved, close and busy. Time passed quickly, but once again lingering fear began to surface. Issues she did not understand that included states rights, slavery and Dred Scott were being discussed by the men in the community. As the popularity of the hotel increased, the number of visitors from around the state and the East also increased. It became more evident that a dark cloud was looming over the country as the issues were not local. Unlike heated discussions of the past, everyone seemed to have an opinion and the conversation often became violent. Could it be that Americans might resort to violence to resolve their differences? The dormant fear of killing was rekindled in Hannah's subconscious mind.

Hannah saw that the married children were more interested in their families than in the affairs of the country. Thurlow seemed to be the most political, considering himself a Democrat and an admirer of Jefferson and Jackson. The other children, except for George Jr., had other things on their minds. It was George Jr. who brought the fear of killing and wars from the subconscious to reality in Hannah. Her oldest son, a risk taker and an adventurer, was not married. These qualities brought about sleepless nights that would grow as the weeks passed.

George W. Strong, along with his family, was adjusting to a new lifestyle, as proprietor of the newest and largest building in Monroe. Captain Strong was never a person to have the luxury of focusing on one thing only. There were always city issues that George would be drawn into. He knew that while he was devoting his time to the Bay, the railroad and the city, Hannah was tending to the children. It had only been in the last few years that he had grown closer to his oldest son. Young George was the proprieter of the hotel but still lived in the shadow of his father. George W., at 61 years of age, was beginning to look upon his children as independent adults, especially George Jr. who was nearing 37.

As George W. Strong looked back on his life, there were few things that he would have done differently. His relationship with his children he felt needed improvement. The hotel seemed to be a step in the right direction as the family was now more closely working together and sharing in a common pursuit: the success of the Strong Hotel. His interests were becoming more focused. The problems of the city, the railroad and politics he thought were behind him. Once again as many times in the past this was not to be.

Civil War

During the 1850s, much of the discussion taking place in Monroe pertained to slavery. A number of articles in the local newspaper followed the events that were taking place in Kansas. A good deal of the information was taken from the *Chicago Tribune* focusing on activities in Kansas, Nebraska and Illinois. The issue of a free state versus a slave state was in dispute. The Missouri Compromise was thought to settle the problem but was not accepted by all. The dispute led to violence and Bloody Kansas. Dred Scott was in the news as the courts tried to resolve the issue of slavery. The court's reversal of its decision did not help. A young man from Connecticut, John Brown, was hanged for trying to arm the slaves. A lady named Harriet Beecher Stowe had written a popular novel, *Uncle Tom's Cabin*, that made Simon Legree a name that became an adjective. Emotions ran high and the country was evenly divided on the issue of slavery. Political parties came apart at the seams. In the early days of Monroe a person was either a Whig or a more popular Democrat.

The Commercial.

M. D. HAMILTON, ... Editor.

MONROE, MICHIGAN.

Thursday, Nov. 8, 1860.

FREEDOM'S STANDARD.

A POLITICAL EARTHQUAKE!

ABRAHAM LINCOLN
Elected President of
the United States.

"Sound the Loud Timbrel."

EVERY NORTHERN STATE FOR LIN-
COLN EXCEPT NEW-JERSEY.

Astonishing Majorities!

DOUGLASISM SQUELCHED!

cuting Attorney, after the latter had publicly withdrawn.

Some of the towns in the County have done most gloriously for the Republican cause, and deserve especial praise. Among them are Ash, Exeter, Bedford, Whiteford, and Summerfield. In 1858 Bedford gave 49 Republican majority. She now has 76. Exeter in 1858 gave 20 Dem. maj. She has this year reduced it to 8. Summerfield in 1858 gave 9 Dem. maj. She now gives 18 Republican, and Whiteford, which gave 57 Rep. in 1858, has increased it to 69.

The vote of this City upon the electoral and State ticket stands as follows:

Republican electors		
" " (First Ward,)		202
" " (Second Ward,)		129
" " (Third Ward,)		48
Total, city,		379
Douglas electors, (First Ward,)		194
" " (Second Ward,)		123
" " (Third Ward,)		53
Total, city,		370
Republican over Douglas,		9

In the Second Ward there were seven votes cast for Breckinridge electors and three in the Third Ward, making the total electoral vote cast 739. The clean Republican gain in the City since the election two years since is FIFTY-EIGHT.

The Democratic majorities on State ticket in the City are as follows:

Barry	6
Fenton	
Francis	6
Farnsworth	
Pennyer	5
Joslyn	5
Sherman	2
Lacey, (Rep.)	2
Willits, (Rep.)	4

Fernando C. Beaman, for Representative in Congress, received 379 votes, and Mr. Coffinberry 383, giving the latter a majority of five votes.

The State Senatorial and Representative vote was as follows:

Mulholland, Senator, (Rep.)		370
Adams, " (Dem.)		392
Stevens, Representative, (Rep.)		374
Choate, " (Dem.)		389

FIRST WARD,

The vote on the County ticket in the City

By 1858 one could be an Abolitionist, a Know Nothing, a version of a Whig or Democrat or a member of a new party that had evolved, the Republicans. The Republicans did not want to eliminate slavery but rather stop its attempt to spread to new states that were being formed in America including Texas, Kansas and Nebraska. The candidate for this new Republican Party was Abraham Lincoln in 1860. He defeated the pro slavery candidate, Douglas, in a close election. The results of the election were also close in Monroe.

On December 20, 1860, in objection to the election South Carolina took the lead in forming the Confederacy with Mississippi, Florida, Alabama, Georgia and Louisiana. The Southerners fired on Fort Sumter against the Union and on April 16, 1861, the war was on. It would take only a short time before 600,000 men would be under arms, all volunteers. Michigan soldiers were among the first to offer their services to the Union Army. No county in the State would be more prompt than Monroe County to offer its soldiers.

The pioneer fathers were now the senior members of the community. The younger generations had not yet asserted themselves. The reaction to events was taking place so quickly that George W. Strong once again was caught up in the whirlwind sweeping over Monroe. He found himself preparing for war although he was in no way political. George did not dwell on the danger of the events that would unfold. Hannah on the other hand was trembling inside and out. The killing was about to take place.

A call to action took place on April 15, 1861, at the Monroe courthouse. The courtroom was filled to capacity and the following committee was formed.

President: Hon. Warner Wing
Secretaries: S. G. Clarke, J. R. Rauch, and T. S. Clarke
Vice Presidents: Hon. Roderick O' Conner, Colonel J. R. Smith, Christopher Bruckner, Capt. A. D. Perkins, Hon. F. Waldorf, Hon. Laurent Durocher, Rev. E. J. Boyd, General Levi S. Humphrey, Dr. Ephraim Adams, Major Gershom T. Bulkey, **Capt. George W. Strong**, Rev. E. J. Boyd, H. B. Marvin, Major Frasey M. Winans

The Committee, through the chairman, Hon. Edward G. Morton, presented a resolution that denounced the South and supported the Union and the Civil War. The organization of a county military began on April 29, 1861. The population of Monroe County was 22,221 and the number of volunteers who would serve was 2,270. By December 1861, Michigan had sent 13 infantry regiments, three cavalry regiments, and five batteries of light artillery, totaling 16,475 officers and enlisted men to the front.

George A. Strong volunteered on January 1, 1862. The Fifteenth Regiment, or the Mulligan Regiment, as it was called, rendezvoused at Monroe with 860 men from Monroe and adjacent counties. The organization of the regiment was completed and was mustered into service on March 20th, 1862. They broke camp one week later and left Monroe amidst enthusiastic cheers and farewells from a very large crowd. Their destination was the army of the southwest under General Grant. Among the officers was Captain George A. Strong in command of Company K. The 15th Infantry proceeded to join the command of General Grant at a little known area near the Tennessee River, called Shiloh. In the gray light of dawn, April 6, a small Confederate reconnaissance discovered the Union army deployed for battle astride the Corinth Road, just a mile beyond the forward Confederate camps. Storming forward, the Confederates found the Union position unfortified. The Confederate attack under Johnston had achieved almost total surprise. By mid-morning, the Confederates seemed within easy reach of victory, overrunning one frontline Union division that included the 15th Infantry and Captain Strong and capturing its camp. However, stiff resistance on the Union's right entangled Johnston's brigades in a savage fight around Shiloh Church. Throughout the day, Johnston's army hammered the Union's right, which gave ground but did not break. Casualties upon this brutal killing ground were immense. Meanwhile, Johnston's flanking attack stalled in front of Sarah Bell's peach orchard and the dense oak thicket labeled the "hornet's nest" by the Confederates. Grant's left flank withstood Confederate assaults for seven crucial hours before being forced to yield ground in the late afternoon. Despite inflicting heavy casualties and seizing ground, the Confederates only drove Grant towards the river, instead of away from it. The Union survivors established a solid front before Pittsburgh Landing and repulsed the last Confederate charge as dusk ended the first day of fighting.

George A. Strong killed at Shiloh

George A. Strong was seriously wounded on the first assault by the Confederate forces as they drove the Union army back from their position. A rebel soldier had him placed in a tent where his wounds were dressed. He remained in the tent until the Union Army drove the Rebels back and the grounds were recaptured by the troops on the next day. He lived wounded and in pain until five days later when he passed away.

The remains of Captain George A. Strong were returned to Monroe on the early train arriving on the morning of April 17, 1862, accompanied by Sergeant Darrah. The funeral took place at two o'clock on the same day. Hannah and George had lost their oldest son. It was ironic that young George had escaped death when the *Helen Strong* sank in a storm only to have fate catch up to him at the age of 38.

Shiloh was one of the pivotal battles of the Civil War. There were 65,000 Union Soldiers and 45,000 Confederate Soldiers in the battle that resulted in the death of 23,742 men. Captain Strong's 15th regiment took the full force of the first attack and was driven back in bloody combat.

Shortly after the death of George A., the family received a letter from the Union regarding back pay owed to George A. Strong. As Hannah read the letter concerning the Union settlement on back pay, her fears were realized and she wondered what tragedy would be next.

George W. Strong began a change in his life that would follow him to his death. His first born and caretaker of his estate had passed away. A void that would never be filled would grow deeper as time passed. He buried his sorrow but the family could see his demeanor had changed. The years passed and the business at the hotel improved and lightened the sorrow for a time. Thomas, now the oldest surviving son, began to emerge as the family's future caretaker. George tried not to look back, but kept the letter from the government regarding back pay as a reminder of the death of his oldest son and the high personal price to pay to preserve the Union and America.

1863 - 1867

The Civil War continued to dominate the news for years. There were over 70 male descendants from the Strongs in Michigan who volunteered for the Union Army. George realized that less than 35 years ago he could have counted the Strongs in Michigan on one hand. Now many extended family members visited the hotel and George W. Strong could only say that he lost a son in the War and then became silent.

The death of George A. Strong was followed by the death of Crisley Diffenbaugh on September 2, 1863. The death was unexpected and began very difficult times for Helen and the three surviving children. Crisley was an engineer in the employment of the Southern Railroad and also held the position of Superintendent of the Machine Shop. Of all the children of George W. Strong, Helen and Crisley were the most social up to that time and had a large number of friends in the community. Mourners came from as far as Adrian to attend the funeral at the Wesley Chapel. It seemed that the mourning was never-ending for the Strong family.

News of the Civil War was foremost in the minds of everyone. The downtown merchants who visited the Strong Hotel to play pool or enjoy a shave and a hair cut often mentioned the latest news on two of its citizens. George A. Custer, a familiar name in Monroe, was recognized in the press for his achievements in the War and was a town hero Dr. C. T. Southworth surprisingly left the city to join the 18th Michigan Regiment in Kentucky. He was a respected family doctor. Events on the battlefield and its resulting death toll were reported weekly in the newspaper until the War neared an end in 1864. The mood of the city was just beginning to brighten. Tragedy was brought to the forefront once again on April 14, 1865, with the assassination of President Lincoln. The dark clouds of the 1860s had not yet run their course.

Monroe, 1866

After the Civil War

A time of healing and forgetting began once again. Business at the hotel was steady during the War and the following years. The conversation of the guests varied. The new Republican Party was becoming more popular. A new generation of citizens was becoming involved in the affairs of the city. Roderick O'Connor, Silas Arnold, Frederick Waldorf and Thomas Doyle were the Mayors of Monroe. Thomas Doyle was a best friend to George A. Strong and a city leader by 1867. This was another sorrowful reminder for George W. Strong of what could have been if his son had lived.

The city was reluctant to pay taxes for the support of the Insane Asylum in Kalamazoo that year. George Strong opposed the extra spending by the city and spoke against the tax. He felt that it was too costly for the few citizens that would ever need the asylum. Little did he realize that the asylum would play a role in the affairs of the Strong family in later years. The tax eventually passed and George could see that his influence in city politics was no longer a factor. His influential voice in the city was sadly coming to an end.

WASHINGTON STREET FIRE of 1868

WASHINGTON STREET, LOOKING NORTH–MONROE, MICH.

Wednesday, March 18, 1868, was yet another tragic day for George W. Strong and his family. Early on that morning, Monroe became victim to the most destructive fire that has ever occurred in the city. The fire broke out in the rear portion of Strong Hotel at about half past one o'clock in the morning and, aided by a strong wind, spread very rapidly. Because of the wind, the bells could be heard for only a short distance; the fire was out of control before George and the citizens were aroused in sufficient numbers to assist fighting the blaze. The muddy streets make it very slow and difficult to get the engines and early firefighting equipment in position to check the flames.

Meanwhile the flames were making rapid headway with the wooden outbuildings in the rear of the hotel, and soon spread to the wooden buildings on the adjoining lots. Trinity Episcopal Church on the south side and Wakefield's Livery Stable on the north, both of wood, were burning and there seemed no hope of saving anything between Washington Street and the alley west of it. It seemed very doubtful the fire could be kept within the limits of Front Street and the public square.

The fire had been raging two or three hours when the wind subsided and the energetic efforts of the Fire Department and citizens kept the fire from destroying the Clarke Hotel and the entire block where the building was located. The hotel was on fire a number of times and its front was badly damaged but not destroyed. The First National Bank Building offered an obstruction to the further progress of the fire northward on Washington Street and the thick and high stone wall of Dansard's building aided the efforts of the firemen to check the progress eastward on Front Street. The block known as Johnson's Block owned by Messrs. Ives, Licht & Co. and Dorsch and Weiss, in which the *Commercial* newspaper office was located and also the First National Bank Building, and a small building between the two occupied by the Merchants' Union Express Co., were the only buildings left standing on the square east of the alley. That the buildings were saved was regarded as little less than a miracle. The early wind blowing the flames gave everyone the idea that the buildings could not be saved, and their contents were mostly removed.

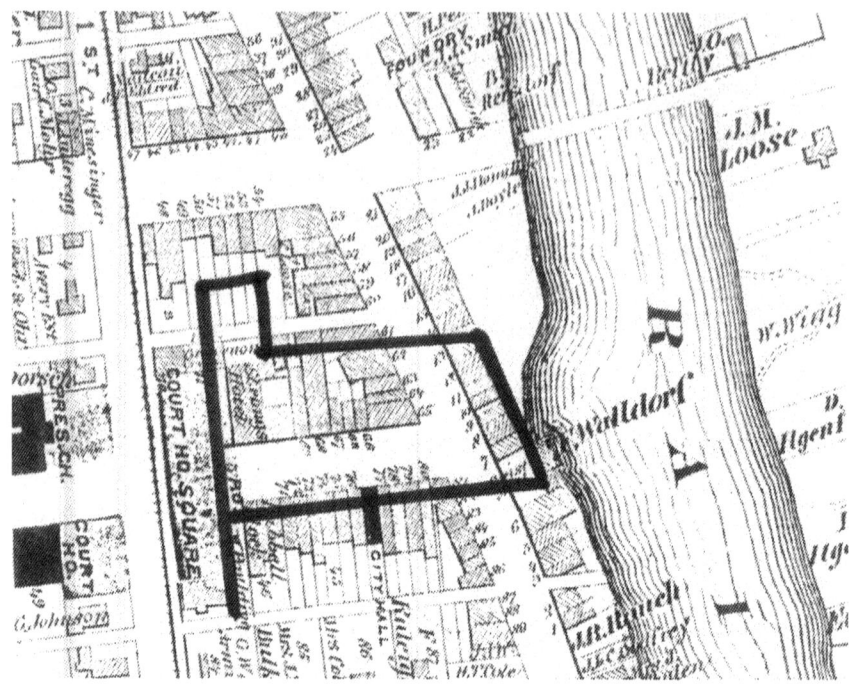

Downtown Monroe area of fire

E. G. Morton's building on Front Street west of the alley was on fire for a considerable time, but was saved in a somewhat damaged condition. Clarke's Hotel around to the east side of Washington Street, a small building adjoining owned by Dr. Arnold and occupied by Miss Augusta Uhl as a fancy store, and the building owned by N. N. Kendal and occupied by him, were considerably damaged by the fire and the heat. Before the wind lulled, the fronts of the buildings east of Washington Street were heavily damaged by the fire and heat and then the fire spread to the block north of Front Street along the River. An almost superhuman exertion by the fire department prevented more destruction.

After the fire was bought under control, it was rumored that an elderly gentleman named Henry Siebke, employed by the Strong Hotel, had perished in the flames.

George W. Strong had to cope with another loss of life as this proved to be true when his remains were found among the debris of the building. While Boyd's building was burning, an oil explosion occurred, throwing the west wall of his building across the alley against Morton's building. The heat became very intense causing great damage to that building.

George W. Strong had made a major financial commitment to the Strong Hotel. A portion of the furniture from the first and second stories was saved, but in damaged condition. The losses were not confined to Strong alone because the guests of the hotel experienced losses in furniture and clothing. The buildings that were completely destroyed were the Strong Hotel, the Post Office building, Wakefield Livery Stable and Consor's Cabinet Store and Shop. Fronting on Washington Street, the fire destroyed the Episcopal Church, W. H. Boyd's old store occupied by Brucker and Powell, and Dansard's stone block two stores, one occupied by J. R. Berry and the other recently made vacant. The loss of property by the fire, without doubt, reached nearly $100,000 while the damage to the businesses could hardly be estimated.

The devastation of the fire was not fully realized until the following day when the citizens awakened to a sad spectacle indeed. The public square, streets and sidewalks were strewn with furniture and goods of every type and confusion reigned supreme. Individuals attempted to find their possessions, and stopping the looting became an overwhelming task. *The Commercial* delayed in publishing a paper, noting much of their type and material was removed from its office and what was not removed was in poor condition. News that was ready for the next issue was rendered meaningless. The cause of the fire was uncertain. A boy who worked for George Strong and had differences concerning his wages was charged and arrested but later released. The fire most likely originated from some other condition, the judge concluded. A dispatch by telegraph was sent to Adrian asking assistance and the city's steam fire engine as quickly as possible but help did not arrive in time. The emergency had passed and their services were not needed when the help arrived. The City of Monroe thanked Chief Bradley from Adrian when he paid a visit on the first train. A few blocks down the street from the blazing buildings on that blustery March night a little girl was propped up in her cradle to watch the spectacle which was burning her father's office. The little girl who recounted the story many times was Jenny

Sawyer.

The citizens quickly began adjusting following the fire. Episcopalians were notified to hold their Friday church and Sabbath meeting in the courthouse. Dr. Sawyer notified his patients he had located his new office over Isaac Lewis's store on Front Street.

The following week *The Commercial* was full of fire sales and removal notices. It was noted that the boy, Nate Williams, who was one of the most active in removing goods from the building, was exonerated. As near as can be determined, the fire was probably started by embers in the ashes. Public sentiment was fully aroused against permitting the building of any sort of wooden structures in the downtown area and even went so far as to demand that any wooden buildings erected in violation of the ordinance be torn down. Two days after the fire, while workmen began pulling down the front wall of the Strong Hotel, it toppled over against the walls of the livery stable, throwing it to the ground and also leveling the wall of the cabinet store. Bills were presented to Common Council for damages. The Council met the following Thursday and Saturday to discuss citizens' demands for adequate water system for pumpers, pulling down walls left standing and the paving of Front Street. Bids were ordered and a wave of rebuilding began in the wake of the fire. Trinity parishioners planned a $10,000 new church but were undecided whether or not to build on the square. Methodists planned a $20,000 edifice on the corner occupied by the parsonage. Mr. Boyd announced he would erect a new store and B. Dansard would also erect two stores. S. B. Wakefield began clearing away the ruins of his stable and went forward with rebuilding. Monroe was coming back to life. Scarcely were the ashes cooled before the enterprising citizens were ready to put their shoulders to the wheel and rebuild. The citizens wanted a better water system to fight fires but it would not come for another 30 years. New emphasis was placed on fire prevention and the citizens were ready to pay the taxes for improvement. It was only a week later that another house burned despite the hand engine getting there in time, and six weeks later the woolen mill burned.

Rebuilding the Hotel

The fire was the most severe financial blow that the Strong family ever experienced. The extent of his ill fortune was not helped by the fact that George W. Strong failed to renew his insurance, causing it to expire. Once again his conservative ways would cause him harm. The money loss was $20,000 with not a dime of insurance on the

property. The 68-year old Strong reverted to the spirit of his younger days and while the bricks were hardly cold, he began arrangements to rebuild the hotel on a larger scale. The property of the Bank of the River Raisin together with the Trinity Episcopal Church property immediately in the rear were purchased. Work began the following spring for a new and modern hotel. Every concerned citizen turned in to push the enterprise and soon the present attractive and new Strong Hotel rose from the ashes of the former building.

In the face of the many disasters which had overtaken Strong, it was a stupendous undertaking, but it was successfully carried out and the new hotel opened auspiciously with Strong and his two sons, William and Thurlow, in charge as landlords and managers. It was an example of the force, determination and perseverance under great discouragement that marked the character of George W. Strong.

The new hotel was opened one year later in 1859 on the site of the old hotel. This gave the new hotel a frontage of 80 feet on Washington Street and 100 feet on the public square. The office in the corner of the building was a continuous room 24 by 34 feet (next to the lobby) and very pleasant. In the rear of this was a sample room 16 by 24 feet, a wash room and a hall leading to the main hall and then to the dining room. The private entrance is on the public square. There a hall 10 feet wide and 40 feet long where it opened into a court in the rear. A stairway led to the upper stories. To the right of this hall were the sample room, wash room and office. To the left was the dining room 33 by 40 feet with windows looking out into the public square. In the rear of the dining room was the kitchen, pantry, laundry, all pleasant and roomy. Fronting on Washington Street on the first floor were three very pleasant stores for rent, one being equipped with a barber shop and connecting with the office of the hotel. Another office was occupied by Luce and Fedfield and another as a telegraph office by the Atlantic and Pacific line. On the second floor with the windows opening both on Washington Street and the public square, were the hotel parlors. There were nearly 50 sleeping rooms for guests in the hotel. Entirely worthy of all praise, the citizens of Monroe marveled at the achievement of Captain Strong following the disaster which seemed almost unparalleled.

Custer's Death - July, 1876

News of the death of George Armstrong Custer reached Monroe on Thursday morning, June 6, 1876. As the news began to sink in, a gloom settled over the Strong Hotel. The following Friday, the City began arrangements for a memorial under the direction of Mayor Spaulding. The bells tolled at four o'clock to mark the beginning of the service at the courthouse. George Strong watched from the hotel as Mayor Spaulding read a dispatch from Washington dated July 6th acknowledging the fall of Custer. He watched quietly as many

Front Street looking west from Washington, 1876.

of his friends including W. H. Boyd, J. M. Bulkley, R. E. Phinney and close friend, Dr. Strong a distant relative made remarks. The following day a steady stream of visitors began coming to Monroe. The hotel overflowed with guests and the death of Custer became a milestone for the Strong Hotel and the City of Monroe.

George did not know Custer well, thinking he was just a young man four years younger than his son, William. Death once again reminded the aging Strong that tragedy was a part of life in this changing land of America.

Industrial Revolution

America was changing quickly as the closing years of the 1800s marked the beginning of the industrial revolution. The rebuilt Strong Hotel opened in 1869 and in a few short decades it would be in need of major renovation. The inventions of Alexander Graham Bell, Henry Ford, Thomas Edison, Andrew Carnegie and Eli Whitney were but a few of the many new modern conveniences that would change America forever. Change would result in a dilemma for Strong as he neared 80 years of age. He found that a tired mind seldom knew which way to turn. Hannah was in poor health and the boys did not seem to have the closeness to a hotel that had become part of George himself. George knew it was time to sell the Strong Hotel.

Population in 1880

City	County	State
4,936	30,111	1,636,937

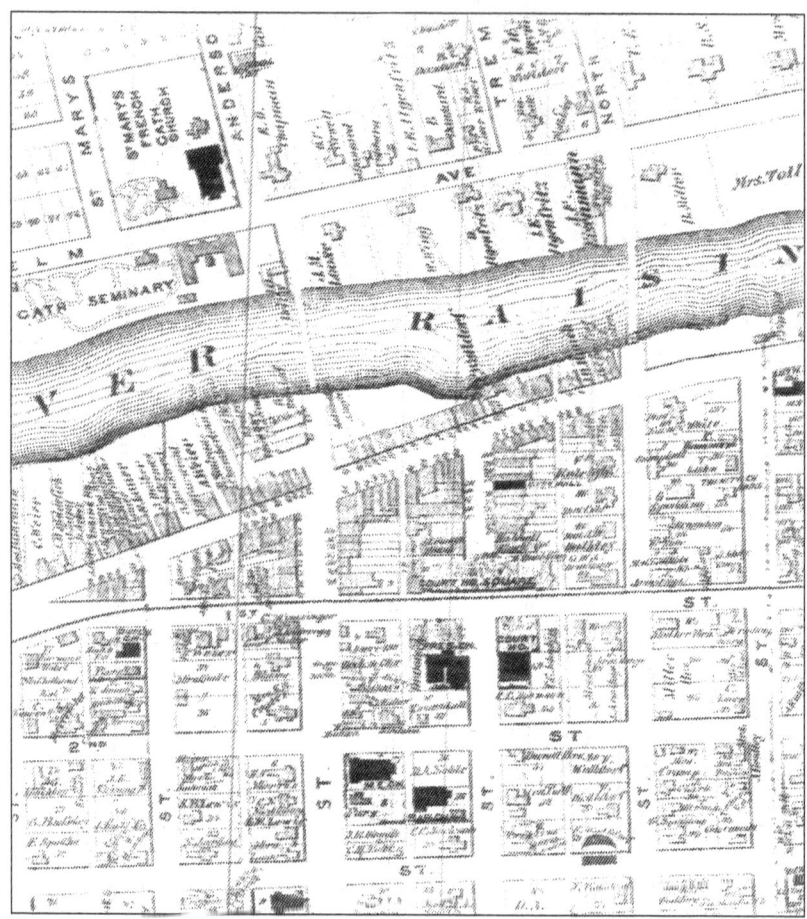

1859 City Map

Mayors of Monroe - Burton Parker 1881-82, Henry Shaw Noble 1883-84, Edwin R. Gilday 1885

The Strong family grew in time as did the city and state. Land was always an important factor in that growth. George W. Strong had narrowed his interest to the management of the hotel. His sons were never confined to one occupation. The variety of business owned by the father contributed to this. Strong did see the value in keeping family investments somewhat organized. As the boys grew older and began investing on their own, the company of G. W. Strong & Sons was formed. Much of the land was under the management of this company.

Liber 70, page 283, dated 1 July 1869, recorded 12 July 1869, **Thomas Strong**, **George W. Strong** and **Hannah** his wife of Monroe, sold to John Naunew, a parcel of land in the city for $865.00, bounded on the North by River Raisin, East by Sole and Dislow warehouse and lot so called now owned by B. F. Morton. South by Front Street, West by Man warehouse, so called now owned by William A. Nobel and being 100 feet in width on said River and Front Street, being the **Strong Warehouse**.

Liber 82, Page 223, dated 19 June 1872, recorded 11 November 1872, **Thomas Strong** sold to D, and W. Line Railroad Co., a parcel of land in the city or $ 350.00. Bounded North by the River Raisin, East by the residue of land of the party of the first part, South by branch of said river and West by the East line of the Stewart farm. The parcel is 143 feet wide from the River Raisin to the South channel of said river, and is from the West side of claim 161.

Liber 54, page 70, dated 16 January 1860, recorded 16 January 1860, George W. Strong sold to **Chrisley Diffenbaugh**, **Thurlow Strong** and **William Strong**, the equal undivided half of a parcel of land situated in the city for $600.00. Bounded Eastwardly by Washington Street, Southerly by lot now belonging to **Chrisley Diffenbaugh** and Hannah Strong, and lot of Allen A. Robinson, held for use of Trinity Church, West by said church lot, lot of Robinson and alley, North by lot of Stephan B. Wakefield. The lot being 50 feet in width on Washington street, and same lot recorded in Liber 52, page 59.

Liber 83, Page 500 dated 16 May 1872, recorded 25 April 1874**, George Diffenbaugh**, estate, **Thomas Strong** gaurdian to George, Lillie and Albert Deffenbaugh minors, sold to **George W. Strong**, at a Public Auction the real estate for $50.00. The undivided on sixth part of in and to the following real estate in the city. Bounded North by land of Stephen B. Wakefield, East by Washington Street, South by land **of George W. Strong** and other occupancy of the Strong Hotel, West by land of Stephan B. Wakefield and an alley being 20 Feet in width on Washington Street.

Liber 82, page 223, dated 19 June 1872, recorded 11 November 1872, **Thomas Strong** sold to D. and W. Line Railroad Co., a parcel of land in the city for $350.00. Bounded North by the River Raisin, East by the residue of land of the party of the first part. South by the South branch of said river and West by the East line of the Stewart farm. The parcel is 143 feet wide from the River Raisin to the South channel of said river, and is from the West side of claim 161.

Liber 82, page 224, dated 19 June 1872, recorded 11 November 1872, **George W. Strong** and wife **Hannah**, sold to the D. and W. Line Railroad Co., a parcel of land in the city 57 feet in width, for $250.00. Bound North by the River Raisin, East by private claim No. 161, South by the South bank of said river and West by the residue of the part owned by the parties of the first part. The 57 feet wide strip is off the East side of the Stewart farm claim No. 543.

Liber 85, page 126, dated 1 October 1872, recorded 27 November 1874, **Thomas Strong** of the city of Monroe, sold to **Thurlow Strong, William Strong** and **Alonzo Strong**, of the same place a parcel of land in the city of Monroe for $1.00. All the undivided three fourth part of the following tract or lot of land. The Southeast comes of lot No. 41 of old village plat East of Monroe Street, according to the recorded plat thereof and being twenty seven and one half feet in front on Washington Street, and forty nine feet deep lying next to the public square and standing in my name but in the trust for said parties of the second part in the proportions of one fourth to me.

Liber 95, page 32, dated 5 March 1877, recorded 5 March 1877, **Thurlow Strong**, of Monroe, sold to Victoria Strong, a parcel of land in the 2nd ward of the city for $1,500.00. The South half of lot No. 98 of old village now city plat East of Monroe Street, according to the recorded plat thereof. The record was signed by **Thurlow Strong.**

Liber 95, page 54, dated 23 April 1877, recorded 23 April 1877, **Thomas Strong**, of Monroe, sold to **William Strong, Thurlow Strong**, of the same place, parcels of land in the city of Monroe, for $1,000.00, described as follows. The hotel property called the Strong Hotel, on lot 41 of old village plat, East of Monroe Street. Bounded North by lot of Calab Lies, East by Washington Street, South by public square, West by alley. Also land of claim No. 166, bounded on North by Front Street, East by land of Milton Terry, called the mill lot. South by First Street and railroad and West by claim No. 161, containing 6 acres, also the island on old claims No. 161 and 166, West by the Canada Southern Railroad.

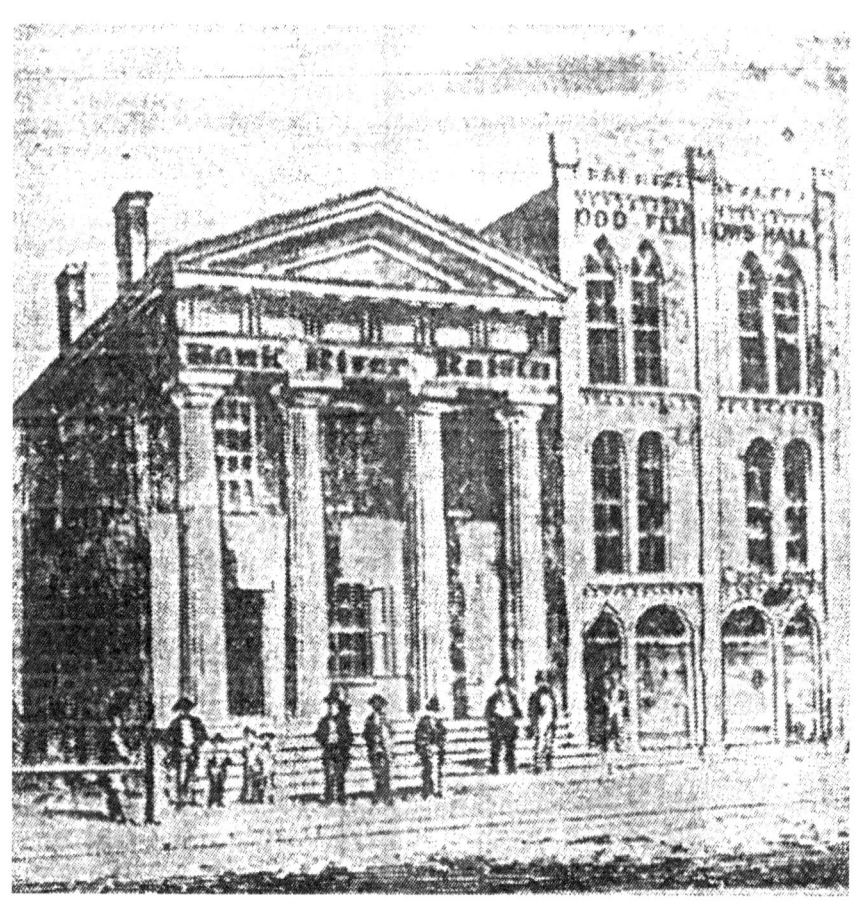

Smith & Clark and G. W. Strong

Prior to 1868, the Strong family managed the properties and the activities at the docks from the former Bank of the River Raisin building. It also housed the post office with room to spare during the 1860s. The brick structure was on the northwest corner of the public park and Washington Street; it was destroyed in the fire of 1868. After the fire the office moved into the new hotel.

William, the youngest son, lived in the hotel even after he married the 23 year old Emma Lewis in 1874. The marriage was witnessed by Joseph Waltman and Lillie Deffenbaugh and performed by Minister D. P. Putnam. William remained one of the proprietors of the Strong Hotel.

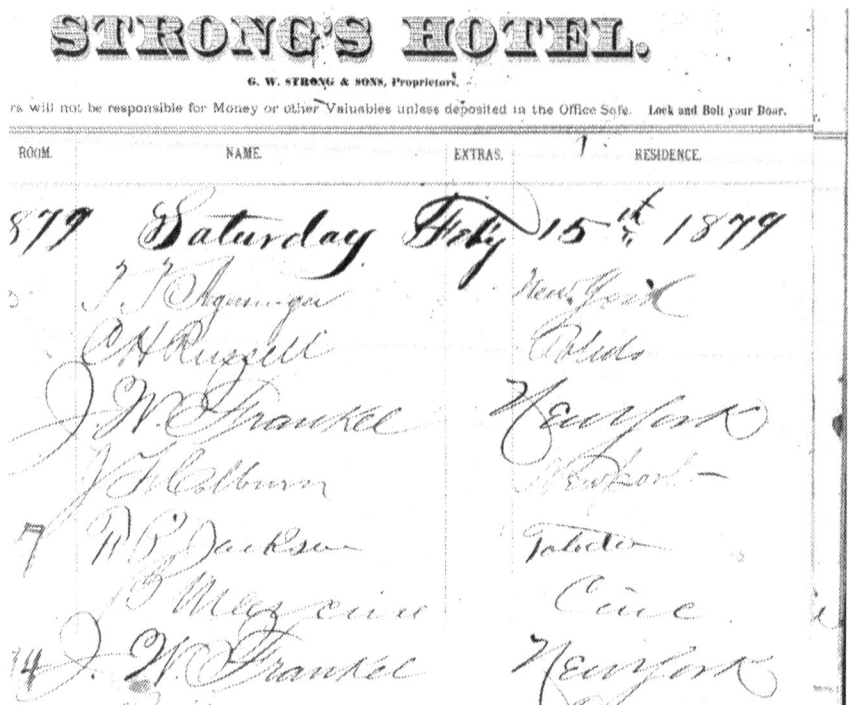

1879 Strong Hotel Register

Business was steady, with a number of established patrons at the hotel. Jacob Hausman was the barber and most noted in town for men's hair needs. Frank Gates ran the billiard parlor, never allowing the patrons to get out of hand. Arnold Phildius was a salesman for Dorsch & Weis. He was a single man who made his home at the hotel. Another older gentleman, Edgar T. Lee dealt in dry goods and seldom left his room. The L.S. & M.S. RR/mail agency was in the hotel run by Thomas Clark. The office of Loose, C. & Sons was adjacent under the supervision of Charles F. Loose. Frank Loose, a speculator, could be found there on occasion. C. W. Hammond, a traveling salesman, would charm the ladies when in town but kept a room in the hotel. Edgar Wilcox was the bookkeeper that occupied one of the rooms. John and William Stoner were always at the hotel but lived on Strong Island and received their orders from George W. Strong. The remaining rooms were filled with guests from every part of America at one time or another.

George spent a good part of the day at the desk tending to the register. Hannah was not able to help as much as in years past. She had become a victim of failing health. As Strong neared 80 years of age, thoughts of selling the hotel became foremost in his mind. Every entry in the register became more difficult to administer.

There was always a Strong who would pass through Monroe. Frank Strong from Boston was one of the many, and the first question George asked was about the relationship to Elder John Strong. News of distant relatives was of great interest as George began spending more time with his memories. His mind frequently drifted to the past which the family thought strange. Every time New York appeared on the register he inquired about his friends in Norfolk who, by now, were deceased. He could remember events that took place in New York more easily than the conversations of yesterday.

George Strong could see that the interest of his children was

1879 Strong Hotel Register

no longer in the hotel. Alonzo went his own way and was never one to take part in the different family businesses. He was very close to his own family and was becoming more Catholic as time passed. Thomas Strong, at the age of 53, married Willhemmenia Schemmer age 28 on November 25, 1980, in Monroe. The marriage by Presbyterian Minister D. H. Putnam was witnessed by brothers Thurlow and William Strong. Thomas, now the eldest son, was a well-known member of the community. He was one of the larger men in the city weighing over 200 pounds and was not in good health. Thomas saw a business opportunity in the many mineral springs in the county. One particular spring was located at LaPlaisance Bay which Thomas turned into a business venture.

Thomas convinced his father to offer a mineral bath to customers at the hotel as a luxury feature. It was out of character for George Strong to agree at nearly 80 years of age however his strong will and independence of the past was withering. Thomas also sold a bottled formula of mineral spirits as one of his many business ventures. Thomas could also see that he had gained influence through his father. Thomas embarked on a business venture that would one day adversely affect George W. Strong in his final years. Thomas was opportunistic and elected to go into the milling business in 1879. He rented a large commercial building on the west side of Monroe Street next to the Monroe Street Bridge. He then converted the building into a flour mill. At the same time, Thomas was elected City Clerk, remaining in that position until his illness and death. His residence was on the corner of Washington and Second Streets one block from the home of Thurlow and two blocks from the Strong Hotel. Willhemmenia, his young wife, assisted at the hotel. Thurlow joined Thomas at the mill and in 1883, like Thomas, followed into city politics becoming Register of Deeds.

Industrial Revolution

The Strong Hotel provided George W. Strong the opportunity to look out an imaginary window and see a nation that was marked by progress. Guests from the East, West, North and South over a twenty year period told of inventions and people that were changing the face of America. The railroad had grown and improved connecting most of the cities in the Midwest and East. Travelers were passing through Monroe from every part of the country. Each had news of progress and change. Freight was traveling by rail taking most of the business from the steamers and canal boats. The exception was railroad barons and workers visiting the hotel. Strong, with a twinkle in his eye, noted that the railroad was a risky business back in his day. George remembered when the iron horse had one or two cars and could hardly be stopped. By 1880, George Westinghouse fixed that with the air brakes and sleeping cars were available thanks to George Pullman. There were dining cars for travelers confirming in Strong's mind rail had reached the ultimate in progress.

To many of the citizens of Monroe, George W. Strong remained "Captain Strong" who never lost his love for the River Raisin and Lake Erie. The railroad did not prevent large freighters loaded with coal and iron ore from servicing the port cities along the Great Lakes. Strong marveled at the size of the new freighters when visiting the port at Toledo. They made his flat bottom boats in 1830 look like a child's toy. A time not so long ago, when there were no railroads or large freighters and the stagecoach was the best way to travel, was the distant past for most Americans. The journey from Vermont to Monroe for the Strong family seemed as if it took place in another world by 1876. A half a century had passed since that journey and the hardships of pioneer Americas were reduced to tales to be told to the grandchildren.

The aging George Strong could not help but be overwhelmed by the increasing number of salesmen who were telling of new products. Iron was used as needed by Strong to build ships and large buildings in pioneer Monroe. Strong found that steel was too costly for construction in his early years. The Bessemer Process made steel affordable. By 1880, salesmen informed Strong that steel was being widely used across America and there was even talk of building a bridge in Brooklyn with its use. Likewise, petroleum use began in 1860 and by 1876 it became an important national product used for light and heat. The fireplace, the task of chopping wood and candle light were no longer essential as new homes made use of petroleum and its byproducts.

The year that George Strong celebrated his 76th birthday, America was celebrating its first 100 years. Foremost on the minds of most hotel guests in 1876 was the world fair in Philadelphia. More than ten million persons helped America celebrate its centennial by visiting the fair. Machine Hall, with its many new inventions, was the main attraction. One of the contest winners at the event was an inventor named Thomas Edison. His inventions of the phonograph and electric light bulb were introduced to America. Another inventor, Alexander Graham Bell, displayed a "speaking telegraph" better known as a telephone. By 1882 there were electric lights in New York and in 1885, a company known as AT & T was formed.

Closer to home, Strong could see both the kitchen table and the hotel dining room being transformed. Invention of the combine turned Kansas, Nebraska and South Dakota into grain producing states. An abundance of grain gave birth to many new byproducts. Wisconsin became a dairy state exporting its products and during the 1870's Gustavue Swift and Philip Armour were shipping fresh meat in refrigerated railcars. Not only was the menu changing at the Strong Hotel, but so was the conversation at the dining table. On occasion,

Strong could overhear conversation concerning the arts in the Old World. The manner in which Franz Liszt was revolutionizing music post Beethoven (who passed away in 1827) and the new operas by Verdi and Bizet were of little interest to Strong.

This was also the case as many of the French impressionist artists were becoming popular. Guests that could read French spoke of the author, Victor Hugo, and the novel, *Les Miserables*. More to Strong's liking was the American novel, *Moby Dick*. Although he had never read the novel, he would inquire about the hardy tale of the sea.

Strong could see that literacy in America had changed significantly as both male and female guests signed the register with ease. There were members in his family that could not read or write well and this was becoming less acceptable. He could also see an increase in guests who were a product of the University of Michigan and the new colleges in Lansing and South Bend. They seemed a cut apart and differed from his children and grandchildren, whose interest was local and parochial. Strong recognized that in the end, it was his hotel and his dream and not that of the children. Expensive modernization over time would be required to keep the dream alive. As each month passed, Strong knew that he was not physically able to meet the demands of the hotel and Hannah could no longer be at his side due to her poor health. What began as the thought of selling the hotel some day was followed by admitting to friends that the Strong Hotel was for sale for the right price. In the end, Strong finally realized the Strong Hotel must be sold.

Sale of Strong Hotel begins in 1879

The sale of the Strong Hotel took place in 1882. This would mark the beginning of ten lost years for the hotel. Those years were called the interim times of the hotel by the citizens of Monroe. This period ended when C. B. Southworth purchased the hotel in 1892 and operated it as the Park Hotel for the next fifty years. He would continue the legacy that George W. Strong had begun.

Liber 101, page 18, dated 16 March 1880, recorded 20 March 1880, **George W.**

Strong, Hannah Strong, Thomas Strong, Thurlow Strong and Victoria his wife, **William Strong** and wife Emma, and **Helen Diffanbaugh**, of the city of Monroe, sold to Willis B. Sink of the city of Monroe, the **Strong Hotel**, property including the building therein and also the furniture in said hotel for $15,000.00 and considerations. Bounded and described as follows, North by store and lot owned and occupied by Rupp and Adams, East by Washington Street, South by the public square and West by alley and being the same premises now occupied by said parties or the first part and known as the **Strong Hotel** property including all the buildings therein. Said property being 82 feet in front on Washington Street, West to alley and 93 feet in width on the alley. There being a jog of eleven feet in the South line. A mortgage of $6,000.00 to C. Mutual Life and Insurance Company, dated April 20, 1877, and 8% interest in which party of the second part is to pay as part of the consideration above named. **Hannah** signed with an X, all others signed the deed.

Liber 101, page 517, recorded 16 October 1880, Benjimin Reisdorf, and Raxas Reisdorf, of Browne Valley, Minnesota, sold to **Thomas F. Strong,** a parcel of land in the city for $ 300.00, situated in the 2nd ward of the city, plus a mortgage of $ 1500.00 the second party assumes and agrees to pay. Also all unpaid taxes on said property.

It was difficult to see W. B. Sink, the new owner of the hotel, change its name to the Park Hotel. Over thirty years of historic times in Monroe were gone as George saw his name removed from the heart of downtown. George would often pass the hotel and notice the changes taking place. It was difficult not to look back, but it was time to move on.

The Park Hotel

W. B. Sink was an investor looking for a quick fortune. He underestimated the effort it would take to manage a successful hotel. He made a few quick and easy changes that did not generate the returns he expected.

W. B. Sink of the Park Hotel, has purchased a beautiful American flag 18 X 10. to hang over that building. He also had the Democratic and Republican streamers either of which will be flung to the breeze with the colors in accordance with the complexion of political mass meetings in the city.

It was known in Monroe that W. B. Sink was a speculator and the fate of the hotel was uncertain. The citizens also knew that illness had befallen Hannah Strong, and George Strong was now one of the older members of the community. The younger generations of residents no longer remembered the pioneer days of Monroe and the efforts of one of its surviving pioneers.

Financial Disaster

Following the sale of the hotel, George W. Strong made a departure from the principles that guided him in the past. He was swayed by the enthusiasm of Thomas, Thurlow and even William taking all the profits from the sale of the hotel and invested in the flour mill. Strong was not fully aware of the changes taking place in America as a result of the Industrial Revolution. Factors such as competition, improved transportation, new machinery and labor were changing rapidly. Strong only remembered how easy it was a half century earlier to be successful in the milling business with his

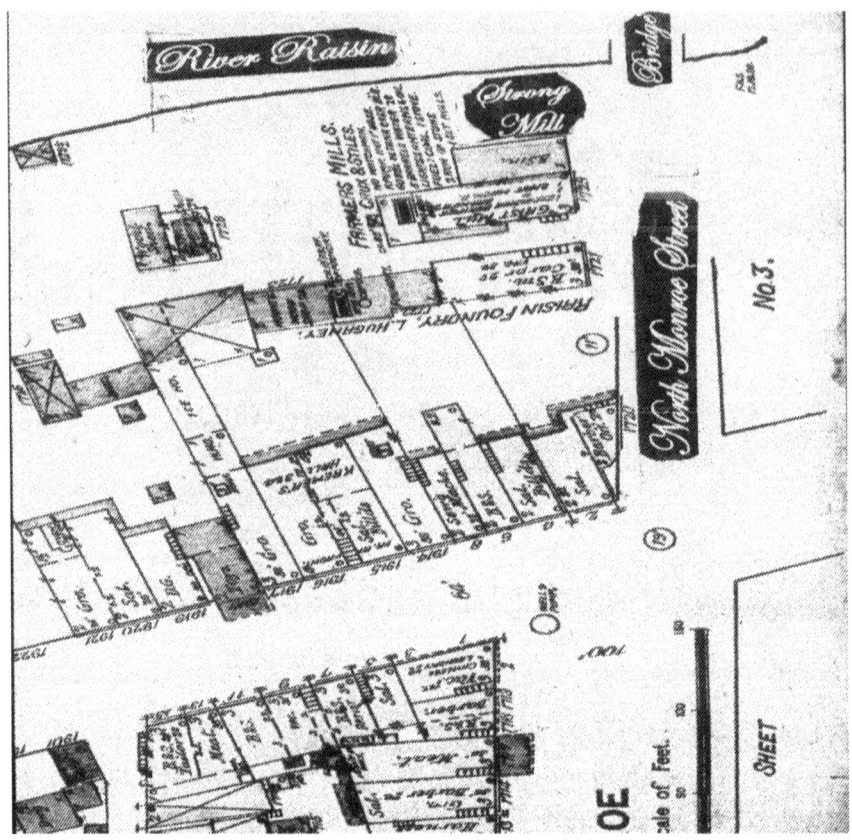

Location of Strong Mill

brother. Changing times and a lack of alertness resulted in the loss of the entire fortune he had accumulated. He took some comfort in the fact that for the time being, he still had his property on the river.

George and Hannah Strong relocated from the former Strong Hotel to a home on the corner of Anderson and Noble Streets. It was the first time they would live on the North side of the River Raisin on what is now North Monroe Street. The flour mill became the property of Caux & Stiles after the losses by the Strong family.

Hotel Changes Hands

Liber 104, page 174, recorded 16 January 1882, Willis B. Sink and wife Eliza, lease the hotel known as the Park Hotel and property to William H. Passware, of Flint, Michigan for the term of five years, commencing 16 January 1882, and ending on the 1st of May 1887, for $2,000.00 per year, payable in twelve equal allotments of $165.60 in advance. At the expiration of this lease said second party is to have the first chance of releasing.

Liber 91, page 357, dated 25 May 1886, recorded 26 May 1886, Willis B. Sink and wife Eliza, sold to Elizabeth W. Walters, and Alderman H. Walters, as tenants in common and both of Monroe, Michigan, the Park Hotel and barn plus all furnishing in the hotel for $14,000.00, plus 7/12 of the taxes paid in December 1886. The interest of said Elizabeth is three fourths of the property herein after and the interest of said Alderman is one fourth. The second party also agrees to assume to pay the sum of $6,000.00 with interest on the sum of from April 20, 1886, at 6% per year to Mortgage held by Mutual Life Insurance Company.

Liber 112, page 653, dated 3 May 1887, recorded 3 May 1887, Alderman H. Walters, leased to Edwin H. Kenrick, on a five year lease his portion of the Park Hotel property for $1,200.00 dollars a year payable $100.00 per month on the 1st day of each and every month during the lease. Also agrees to immediately repair and renew said plumbing during the lease. It includes the steam boiler and pumps. Bath tubs upstairs and down. Water tanks in both bathrooms and water closets and all pumps and appurtenance of or belonging to same, The lease starts 1 May 1887.

Liber 91, page 447, dated 3 January 1891, recorded 5 January 1891, Alderman H. Walters and wife and Thomas R, Waters and his wife of Monroe, Michigan, sold to Edwin H. Kenrick, of the same place the Park Hotel property and buildings and furniture for $14,500.00 dollars.

Population in 1890

City	County	State
5,258	32,337	2,093,890

Clinton B. Southworth leases Park Hotel

Clinton B. Southworth was born in 1868 which was near the time the Strong Hotel was being rebuilt following the fire that ravaged downtown Monroe. His father, a very successful doctor in Monroe passed away when Clinton was 16. Clinton B. Southworth was a

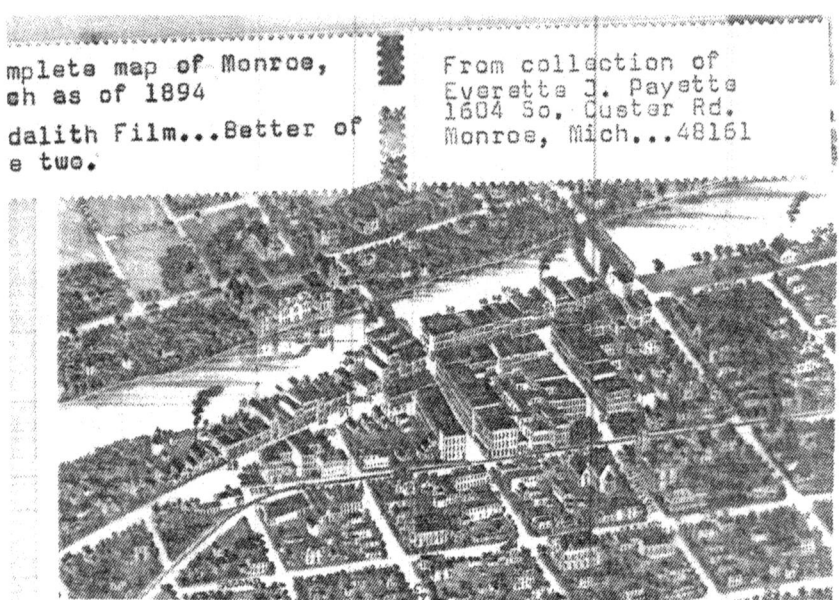

The City in 1894

successful and well-known young man in Monroe when he and a
partner leased the Park Hotel. At the age of 24, Southworth was the
new manager and in time, the new owner of the Park Hotel for the
next 50 years.

Liber 118, page 604, dated 17 December 1892, recorded 6 January 1893, Edwin
H. Kenrick, a the year lease to **Clinton B. Southworth**, of Frenchtown, and
Frederick S. Osgood, of Toledo, Ohio, the Park Hotel property, Parties of the
second part are to take possession of said premises 1 January 1893, and repairs
to the building and any painting and decorating which may be found necessary
during the lease without any expense or cost to said party of the first part, The
lease is $2,000.00 dollars a year payable in advance on 1 January every year of
the lease. Also maintaining the insurance of the said lease premises for the sum of
$10,000.00 dollars against loss or damage by fire.

Liber 122, page 394, dated 24 December 1894, recorded 29 December 1984, this
agreement made by and between Charles Wright and Herman Q. Strasburg of
Detroit, Michigan, holder and owners of a certain lease and contract dated 17
December 1892, given by Edwin H. Kenrick, to **Clinton B. Southworth**, and
Frederick S. Osgood, and now held by said **Southworth** and Mallie M. Stevens,
assignee of said Osgood. Parties of the first part and Alderman H. Waters and
Thomas T, Waters of Monroe, Michigan, for a good and valuable consideration
by said first parties duly received further consideration of one dollar to said first

parties, transferred and set over by these present do grant a bargain sell, assign transfer and set over unto the said parties of the second part, a certain lease and contract.

Liber 154, page 24, dated 16 March 1904, recorded 16 May 1904, Alderman H. Waters, his last will and testament. To Alice Kendal, Thomas T. Waters, Robert D. Waters, William Hanson and Mrs. Callahan, each gets $10,000.00 dollars, To Clinton B. **Southworth** and his wife $1,000.00 dollars each. All the remainder of my estate real and personal, I bequeath to Arthur L, Hanson of Detroit, Michigan, and hereby revoke any former will,

Liber 165, page 156, dated 1 May 1908, recorded 1 May 1908, Arthur L. Hanson, and wife Esteele B. Hanson, of Monroe, Michigan, sold to Thomas T, Waters, of the same place the undivided one half of the Park Hotel property and all his interests in the furniture, fixtures and outfit of said Park Hotel, and also the post office fixtures therein. Excepting a certain lease and contract given by said Thomas T, Waters and Alderman H. Waters, to Clinton B. Southworth, on the 1st day of May 1900. This is not recorded in the land records.

Clinton B. Southworth buys Park Hotel

Liber 171, page 396, 31 May 1911, recorded 31 May 1911, Thomas R. Waters and wife Kora, of the city of Monroe, Michigan, sold to Clinton B. Southworth, and wife Philey E. Southworth, of the same place, the Park Hotel property for $20,000.

The population of Monroe had settled and the growth years had passed. Clinton B. Southworth would weather difficult years to make the Park Hotel once again famous and profitable.

Charles Byron Southworth who purchased the hotel in 1892 was the "host of Monroe" for more than 50 years. Famous guests included Henry Ford, Mrs. George Custer, and presidents; William Howard Taft and Theodore Roosevelt. Charles Byron Southworth was the son of Dr. Charles Tracy Southworth.

Chapter 10 - The Final Years of George W. Strong

Doctor Southworth

Doctor Charles Tracy Southworth was the son of a doctor and was born in New York in 1827. He was the same age as Thomas Strong. Dr. Southworth had moved to Monroe at the age of 16. He received his education at Oberlin, Ohio and at the University of Michigan. He attended his first course of medical lectures at the College of Physicians and Surgeons at New York in 1845. He then went to Paris where he took a course under Ricord and Trousseau, then spent two years interning at a hospital in Madrid, Spain, graduating at the University of Madrid in May, 1846. That year he went to Havana, Cuba, where he practiced until March, 1851. His next stop was Matamoras, Mexico, then on to Vera Cruz. In April, 1853, he was commissioned Division Surgeon of the Cavalry by General Santa Anna on his return to Mexico. The Dictator accompanied him to Mexico City. He resigned from his position when Santa Anna abdicated and in 1856 was appointed Surgeon General of the Army of the North by Santiago Vidaurri, then governor and commander-in-chief of forces of Coahuila and Nueva Leon. In 1857, he resigned the commission of Vidaurri, and returned to Mexico City. He left Mexico by way of Acapulco and arrived in Monroe, Michigan, January 5, 1859. He married Frances H. Blankekee who died in 1865, leaving him two daughters. In 1863, a year after the death of Captain George A. Strong, Dr. Southworth was commissioned surgeon of the Eighteenth Michigan Volunteer Infantry, but resigned his commission, June, 1864, due to ill health. In September, 1865, he was married to Eliza Jane Clark, with whom he had two sons and a daughter. It was in 1880 that he was called on to attend to the failing health of Hannah Strong.

Death of Hannah Strong

Time had taken its toll on Hannah Strong prior to the sale of the hotel. The family noticed a difference in Hannah beginning in 1876. She later came under the care of Dr. Southworth but her health continued to deteriorate. Dr. Southworth could do little for her during the winter of 1882. George spent that winter closer to Hannah than he had been for many years. Prior to her illness, he often neglected her, taking her for granted. It seemed to have begun in New York with the trip West. It followed during one business venture after another in Monroe. Hannah never complained as she raised the children in George's absence. He was fortunate that she was a caring and giving person many times in the past. The boys, like their father, were never as close to their mother as Helen. They did not visit often even in her final months. The boys were distracted by city politics and business. In that respect, they were not unlike their father. George Strong was thankful for Helen, his only daughter. She was always there and knew what to do to make her mother comfortable. Death came on Thursday, April 19, 1883, for Hannah Strong.

George looked at the resting body of his wife remembering he had experienced the death of his son, passengers on his ships and many of his close friends before her. He had survived the disaster at the hotel, financial losses and many storms on the lakes. The service for Hannah was held on the Sunday following her death in their new home in the Fourth Ward and the rapidly developing North side of the River Raisin. They had been in the home for only three short years and George would not remember them as enjoyable years due to Hannah's illness. Many of the town's most prominent families came to the home to express their condolences to the family. They all knew Hannah for what she was. The community regarded her as a charitable, kind, open-handed and hospitable woman. The funeral service was conducted by Reverends Macomber and Mattoon. A funeral procession followed along Monroe Street, then West on Fifth Street to Woodland Cemetery. Hannah was laid to rest in the family plot next to the grave of her son, George A. Strong. The following year, Dr. Southworth passed away as a result of a heart injury caused by a runaway team colliding into his carriage from behind while he was on his way to Maybee. His son, Clinton Byron Southworth, was 16 at the time and an admirer of Strong.

1884 Centennial - Monroe's first 100 years

The grandest celebration of the day in Michigan

20,000 strangers in city

George W. Strong was going through a period of adjustment in 1884. He was living alone, tending to himself well on some days and neglectful on others. More often than not, he would allow himself to fall into a disheveled and unkempt state. The citizens began to note the change in the once daunting Captain. The children began paying special attention to their father in June and July of 1884. He was to be a special guest at the celebration of the Centennial Celebration of the City of Monroe. On the day of the celebration, George W. Strong had a sharp mind and looked the man he once was.

The events of the day were best described in the *Monroe Democrat* on July 10, 1884:

"Though the day dawned very gloomily and inauspiciously with a rain storm that threatened to be long-lived, the Fourth of July, 1884 was one that will long be remembered with pride the people of Monroe , and with pleasure by the thoughts of visitors who helped us celebrate it. Considerable uneasiness was felt in the morning as to what would be the program of the weather bureau for the day, but by 8 o'clock it was settled that we should have as lovely a day for our celebration as could have been made to order. It had rained enough to lay the dust, and the storms which prevailed us made the air cool. As early as five o'clock, and when the outlook was most gloomy, people began arriving from the country, and by seven o'clock the streets presented a lively appearance. The stream of teams continued to pour into town till every garn, shed yard and other available place for stabling was occupied, and it seemed as if at least half of the county had turned out. With the arrival of the first train the crowd was very perceptibly increased, and each subsequent arrival brought its hundreds of visitors. In fact several hundred came Thursday to be on hand early Friday morning. The regular train from the west brought six coaches packed full, and an hour later a special arrived with five freight cars and three cabooses jammed full inside and out. Besides these many were left at the way station because of the over-crowded condition of the cars. The western people were naturally indignant at the kind and extent of the accommodations furnished them by the railroad company as there was no extraordinary demand upon its passenger traffic that day. ....

hotel, restaurants and business places generally were full to overflowing. The visitors found the city decorated as it never was before. There was scarcely a business place, or a dwelling near the center of the city, that did not remind the observer that an event of more than ordinary importance was at hand, while the decorations of some buildings were elaborate and beautiful. Two large arches of welcome spanning Monroe and Washington Streets; large banners floated over the streets while a large steamer bearing the inscription, "Welcome Comrades," stretched across Monroe Street captured the veterans. The streets were lined with small trees and burghs, and Monroe fully maintained her reputation as the Floral City. The residence of Dr. Sawyer which stands upon the site of Winchester's headquarters was handsomely decorated, and a good sized sketch of the headquarters hung over the front gate. The houses along the line of march also profusely decorated. The forenoon was devoted to the reception of guests and visiting organizations and escorting the latter to their respective headquarters. At 11:45 the Monroe band marched to the headquarters to the reception committee in the city hall and escorted the speakers, guests and officers of the day to the court house square, where upon a large stand beautifully trimmed the exercises of the forenoon were held. Across the front in large letters was the work "greeting:" at the left of it was 1784: at the right 1884. Behind the president of the day, Mayor Noble, and the speakers we noticed upon the platform Prof. Ford, H. A. Wilkerson, Ezra Lockwood, A. F. Roberts, C. Hertzler, Charles Knap, John Doyle, H. B. Hurd, Rev. Pratt and Cobern, Dr. Sawyer, **G. W. Strong**, J. M. Sterling, W. A. Nobel, T. E. Wing, and several others. The ceremonies began with music by the Monroe cornet band, which was followed by an eloquent address of welcome by Mayor Noble. The band rendered another selection and Rev. Pratt offered a brief prayer. After the singing of he Star Spangled Banner, Mayor Noble introduced Rev. Frank O'Brien, who delivered the opening address. He said: "In the name of the people of Monroe I extend to you all a welcome as hearty and generous as their hospitality. These are not idle words, but are spoken in all sincerity. To the Monroe man belongs the glad consciousness that he has for his home the most beautiful spot in all the country. If you would fully appreciate her beauties you must go away from home. She has furnished the nation more brave soldiers and able, honest statesmen that any other city of her size.

The speakers reviewed the history of the place from its settlement, paid a flattering compliment to the French, and said: "that as the first settlers had a Black Robe to welcome them to the shores of the Raisin, it is well that you should have one to welcome you today." After music by the Carleton band, Mayor Nobel introduced Judge Christiancy, who most cordially received by the audience. It was with considerable effort that he read his address, and he completely broke down when he referred to his early life in Monroe. He was frequently applauded in the course of his remarks, which were as follows:

From my native place in Montgomery county, N. Y. Forty-five years ago I came to Monroe to deliver a speech here, and I come now again to Monroe to deliver my last. And though now practically a stranger to most of the people of this city and the county of Monroe, I am reluctant to entertain the thought that I can ever be a stranger here where the best years of my manhood were spent, from the age of 21 to the that of 62; where grew up the social intercourse, the strong attachments, and the friendly and endearing relations which have become a part of my existence. For over twenty years I knew every man, woman and child in this city and they knew me. I was after that more secluded by my official duties, and have been ten years absent. A new generation has grown up. Comparatively few remain whose faces are yet familiar, and these are mostly younger than myself, and upon these, as upon myself, time has begun to engrave his lines, and to powder their heads with snow. And yet it seems bur a little while since, on the 19th of May 1836, at the age of 24, I landed at the wharf from the old steamer General Jackson to work out my life's destiny among strangers, and in a land to me then strange. This then was 48 years ago, nearly half the period which has elapsed since the first white man settled on the bands of the River Raisin. How well I remember the people I found here at that time. If time would permit I would be glad to speak of all these, as well as those who came for years after, but I must confine myself to a few of the more prominent here when I came. In the legal profession I found Wing & Noble (Warner Wing and David A. Noble) Aspheus Felch, Robert McClelland and Jefferson G. Thurber: among the practicing physicians, Dr. Robert Clark, Dr. Adams, Dr. Landon and Smith. Among the merchants, Merill & Whittier, Wm. H. Boyd, Wm. V. Studdiford, Roderick O'Conner, Roberts & Armitage, James Hale, and Horatio Conant (druggist). Among the other leading men of influence or enterprise Dan B. Miller, Teba Murphy, Daniel s. Bacon, Austin E. Wing, Oliver Johnson, Levi S. Humphrey, Wolcott Lawrence, Col. Anderson, Charles Nobel, Daniel Nobel, Thomas G. Cole, James J. Godfroy, Joseph Loranger, Laurent Durocher, George B. Harleston, Isaac Lewis, **Geo. W. Strong**, Allen A. Radineau, James Q. Adams, Julius D. Morton, Gersham T. Bulkey, Col. Peter P. Ferry. **Of these only six, as far as I can learn, remains alive. Alpheus Felch, William H. Boyd, James Armitage, Isaac Lewis, Allen A. Rabineau and Geo. W. Strong. ......"**

It was a moment of glory for the Strong family.

1879 Strong Hotel Register Sketch

Aging George W. Strong

Reading the newspaper became a favorite pastime for the visibly subdued and now quiet George Strong. Reading would lapse into blank stares at the printed page of the newspaper for minutes then hours. Dozing and naps were becoming more frequent. A natural talent that remained with Strong to the end was his ability to sketch. Over the years he sketched maps through the wilderness, boats, warehouses, stores, homes and a massive hotel. His sketches in the end were an attempt to capture memories of the past. His sketches survived but the memories that helped create them were fleeting.

The days at LaPlaisance Bay seemed to be the best of the old days. His companion became his thoughts of yesteryear. Although the family had grown to 17 grandchildren and 9 great-grandchildren, the occasional visits seemed too infrequent to suit an increasingly lonely pioneer of almost a century ago. The grandchildren reveled in the tales of pioneer Monroe. A favorite story for the children concerned the Indians:

"Back in the old days, Indian relics were plentiful at LaPlaisance Bay and the River. Every time we turned over ground, relics were found. One of the strangest finds was a bushel of roasted corn in the ear. It was taken from a depth of thirty feet while digging a grave. The corn lay beneath a layer of sand. The cobs were so decayed that they crumbled when they were disturbed. The kernels surprising were nearly perfect in shape although charred. Then an old Indian helped us solve the mystery of the corn. The Indians raised the corn, charred it and buried it marking the location. They made sure it was buried below the reach of animals and the frost. The corn would remain edible for as long as fifty years. When the tribe or hunting parties returned to the area there would be a ready meal waiting for them."

The children enjoyed the tale but noticed that a forgetful grandfather would tell the same story over and over again. The children became reluctant to visit because grandfather was becoming redundant. The family took this lightly thinking George W. Strong was just getting old.

The Fourth Ward and the home of George W. Strong were near the former home of Captain Smith and Elvira. Strong often thought of his early days in Monroe and his association with the Smith family. Those memories were reinforced each time he neared the house and crossed the bridge to the center of town. I. E. Ilfenfritz arrived in Monroe in 1847 and established a family nursery which grew into one of the most profitable businesses in Monroe. His first home was the old Navarre-Anderson trading post which he remodeled and used

175

until buying the Smith home in 1872. Elvira Smith left Monroe that year and moved back to her family home in Watertown, New York. There she remarried before she passed away in November, 1878.

Along with old age, confusion began to overtake Strong. He would stop at the Smith home and ask to see Elvira. Mrs. Ilgenfritz would try to explain that Elvira moved away some time ago and had since passed away. Each time this would occur, George Strong would be a bit more defiant and resistant in understanding what the Ilgenfritz family was telling him. In turn, the children of George Strong began to realize that something was happening to their father. He seemed to be in good health but his mind was playing tricks on him.

1879 Strong Hotel Register Sketches

The task of watching his father more closely was assigned to William Strong who also lived in the Fourth Ward at 1212 East Elm Street. William, thinking of his father's safety, no longer would allow George Strong to drive his team and wagon or ride his horses. This did not prevent George Strong from being mobile. He would walk to town often forgetting his way back home. The residences of the City of Monroe now began to recognize that one of the oldest pioneer fathers of the city was not mentally stable.

William was notified one afternoon that George Strong was wading in the middle of the river. William carefully made his way

1879 Strong Hotel Register Sketch

to his father and attempted to instruct him to return to shore. George Strong resisted, explaining he was going to Strong Field where a carnival was held and then he would proceed to the docks. William tried to explain that there was no carnival and no longer any activity at the docks. Finally William tried to forcefully get his father to return to shore only to find that Strong forcefully resisted.

It was only after long minutes of guarded conversation, that George Strong returned home. George W. Strong did have occasional calm periods and was comfortable around company as he neared 90 years of age. Thomas, Helen and especially Thurlow realized what a milestone it was to reach 90 years of age. It was an occasion for the family to plan a 90th birthday party on April 10, 1890. The planning and excitement for the occasion developed a momentum of its own. It became a social event in the City attended by family, friends and those few who had a historic perspective of the city. The gathering of all the Strong children, including Alonzo, provided an occasion to discuss the fate of their father. It was determined to make changes in the ownership of property while their father was somewhat cooperative.

Liber 125, page 559, dated 7 March 1890, recorded 7 March 1890, **George W. Strong**, of the city of Monroe, sold to **Thurlow A. Strong**, of the same place, a parcel of land in the 3rd Ward of the city for $1.00 dollar, bounded North by the bayou or South banch of the River Raisin, East by remaining land of the first part on the South Front Street in said city, and on the West by of Vital Willet, and being a part of claim 161.

Liber 116, page 627, dated 23 April 1890, recorded 2 May 1890, **George W. Strong**, sold to **Thurlow A. Strong,** for $1.00 Dollar a parcel of land in the 3rd ward, known as the Strong homestead premise, containing 25 acres more or less. All mortgage on said land and premises held and said Hannah Strong in her lifetime.

The five surviving children of George W. Strong were now elderly themselves and in some cases not in good health. They were busy with their own families and professions. They were not yet ready for a decision on a caretaker for their father. Helen was a widow and felt she alone could not care for her father. Thomas was in very poor health and needed care himself. Victoria, the wife of Thurlow, had considerable social status in the community due to her Godfroy ancestors and discouraged Thurlow from becoming overly involved. William, who had been caring for his father, wished to share the burden. It was not an option to ask Alonzo, who was estranged from the family.

The final decision was to let time take its course.

Last days of George W. Strong

The glory years for George Strong were now far in the past and had not taken place in the lifetime of most of the citizens of Monroe. The city became a settled community with new generations of citizens. It was increasingly difficult to keep Strong confined and away from the city. He spoke harshly to the people that no longer remembered the pioneer days of Monroe. He was tolerated but no longer respected as he attempted to revisit the sites he had once an important part in building. He became defensive and physical when a store owner or barber would ask him to move on. Unable to remember his way home, the children often were called to assist. He would not accept advice or corrections to his misrepresentation. His life became less and less structured. Eating and sleeping became intermittent. He began to forcefully resist any attempts to alter his lifestyle. There was no known cure for his condition.

1891

A series of tragedies followed in a short period of time. Another member of a noted pioneer family passed away in 1891. George W. Strong accompanied by family members, attended the funeral of Joseph M. Sterling on May 18th, 1891. Joseph Sterling was 73 years of age and a member of one of the most notable of the pioneer families of historical Monroe.

Following the death of Sterling would be the death of George Strong's oldest son, Thomas, who had been ill for some time. On July 30, 1891 George W. Strong could no longer relate to tragedy of a death in the family. Thomas Strong was a very popular city clerk at the time of his death. He had been in poor health for some time and experienced a fractured hernia which led to his death. When his condition worsened, he was operated on in an attempt to cure him. The operation on the hernia was successful but Thomas in his weakened condition failed to rally and passed away shortly after. His death marked the passing of another member of one of the best known families of the era.

There were now four surviving children to deal with their father's condition. Helen at 66 years of age was the oldest child and William at 58 was the youngest.

The confused condition of George W. Strong continued. The doctors of that time did not have the medical expertise on treating the symptoms and conditions related to aging. It would be left to the family to determine the best course of action for their aging father. Full time care by family members would be too demanding as George became more and more unruly. All his assets and possessions were transferred or sold in anticipation of the problems that the family was expecting. The man who once was among the largest landowners in the city, a captain with a fleet of ships, the builder of a railroad and the proud owner of the Strong Hotel now had no possessions and a

Complete map of Monroe, Mich as of 1894

Kodalith Film...Better of the two.

From collection of Everette J. Payette 1604 So. Custer Rd. Monroe, Mich...48161

The City in 1894

failing mind. A final judgment by the courts took place in 1891 when the children determined to declare their father violently insane.

An exile began as George W. Strong was destined to be committed to an asylum in Kalamazoo, Michigan, the institution he thought would be of little use and years earlier would not support with his taxes.

Legally Violently Insane

Courthouse at the corner of Washington and Second Sts., 1895

The children had the option of committing their father to the county home in Monroe located on Raisinville Road. It was a home for the feeble minded and indigents. This option was disregarded in favor of the asylum in Kalamazoo, Michigan.

On the 27th day of October, 1891, George Diffenbaugh, Grandson of George W. Strong and son of daughter Helen, petitioned Judge

Odell Dunbar and the Court of Monroe to declare George W. Strong insane.

It was noted to the court that George W. Strong had no estate and no personal items of value; a fee of $20.00 would be given monthly for miscellaneous asylum expenses.

The petition requested that George W. Strong be admitted to the asylum for the insane in Kalamazoo, Michigan, and thereafter supported as a private patient as required under said statues of the State of Michigan. There are many records in the office of the Register of Deeds concerning the properties owned by George W. Strong. There is only one document in Probate Court referring to the same. As best as can be translated from these documents is the following:

State of Michigan County of Monroe at a session of the Court held at the Probate Office in the city of Monroe on Thursday the 27th Day of October 1891.
present Addison Dunbar, Judge of Probate
In the matter of **George W. Strong** *an alleged insane person*
On reading and filing the application of **George Diffenbaugh**
in behalf of said **George W. Strong** *praying that he be admitted to the Michigan asylum for the insane as an insane person, therefore to be supported at private expense. It is ordered that Wednesday, the 28th day of October 1891 at 8 o'clock in the fornoon, at the Probate office in the city of Monroe be the assigned the hearing of application and that notice of application, and of the time and place of hearing thereof be given to said* **George W. Strong** *and also to* **Thurlow A., William and Alonzo Strong and Helen Diffenbaugh** *relatives of* **George W. Strong** *by service of a copy of service of this order personally on each of them to show cause, if any, why the prayer of said application should not be granted.*

State of Michigan County of Monroe Addison Dunbar Judge of Probate Court in the matter of appointing a guardian of George W. Strong, an alleged insane person
Your petition would respectfully represent to the Court that he is a

son of George W. Strong that said George Strong is of the age of 91 years and a resident of said county and has no estate but is a pensioner of a monthly payment of twenty dollars or thereabout as your petition is informed and verifiably believes

Your petitioner whither represents that it is necessary that a guardian be appointed of the person and estate of said George W. Strong for the following specified reason vis: P. T. that said George W. Strong was declared insane in this court and ordered to conveyed to the Michigan insane asylum on October 28, 1891 as a private patient and no person is qualified to draw said person out unless a guardian is appointed.

Your petition further requests that names and relationship of next of kin of said George W. Strong and other persons interested in said estate of your petition is informed and believes, are as follows:
Said guardian to be Helen Diffenbaugh

Helen Diffenbaugh, Daughter
William Strong Son
Alonzo Strong Son
Thurlow Strong Son
Helen Strong Grandchild - child of deceased Thomas
Lazetta Strong Grandchild - child of deceased Thomas
Lillian Strong Grandchild - child of deceased Thomas
Thomas Strong Grandchild - child of deceased Thomas
Sherman Strong Grandchild - child of deceased Thomas
Oscar Strong Grandchild - child of deceased Thomas

Two statements were furnished as testimony to the insanity of George W. Strong.

Testimony
Henry R. Austin being duly sworn and says that he resides in the city of Monroe 57 years of age. Acquainted with G. W. Strong and

has been for 30 years

Question: Do you believe him insane?
Henry Austin: I do
Question: What is your reason for believing him insane?
Henry Austin: His manner and incoherent speech
Question: you are sure p. m.?
Henry Austin: I am
Question: What time was the time he was so bad?
Henry Austin: One day last week
Question: Do you believe him dangerous?
Henry Austin: Yes, for a man in his feeble condition
Further deposement with not.

Henry Root Austin, born in 1834, was well-educated and taught school at Jackson, Michigan and at the University of Michigan in his early years. He enlisted in the Union Army during the Civil War and following the War he began an active business venture in Monroe where he became closely acquainted with George W. Strong. In 1868, Mr. Austin formed a partnership with Frank H. Hubbard and William H. Boyd in the wholesale and retail mercantile business in Monroe. He left the mercantile business in 1873 and entered the rail mail business where he remained active in that business for 15 years. He was appointed Postmaster in 1891 and held that position when George W. Strong was committed.

Testimony
E. F. Hubble being duly sworn and deposed says that he is 50 years old and upwards and is acquainted in George W. Strong ever since boyhood
Question: Do you believe him insane?
E. R. Hubble: *yes*
Question: What is your reason for believing him insane?
E. R. Hubble: *From his acts*
Question: Can you state what in violation------------------ ?

E. R. Hubble: *Within a month in relation to Cleveland he was going to stop in Monroe and also in purchasing land*
Question*: Do you believe him dangerous?*
E. R. Hubble: *Yes considering his age and feebleness*
Further deposement with not.

Erastus Hubble was the son of Nathan Hubble who was one of the early sheriffs and surveyors of Monroe and was landlord of the American House. This building stood on the corner of Front and Monroe Streets and was a stop for the stagecoach and travelers.
Erastus was a well-known stage driver and was known for dramatic adventures in the early stagecoach days. He was marshal of Monroe in 1879, 1880 and 1881. Thurlow Strong was Justice of the Peace in 1879 and represented the Second Ward in 1881. Thomas Doyle was also active in city politics at the time.

All that now remained for George W. Strong was the final train ride to the asylum for the insane in Kalamazoo, Michigan. Family members accompanied the man who was not to die the death of a pioneer hero but bound to the fate of souls lost in a forgotten past.
It took only four short months for his journey to end in the asylum and mark the end of the first pioneer of the Park Hotel.

Monroe Democrat **Thursday, Oct. 29, 1891**
"Capt. Geo. W. Strong who has been gradually losing his mind for some time, became violently insane and unmanageable. He was taken to the asylum at Kalamazoo yesterday morning. A great deal of sympathy is expressed at the captain's affliction in his advanced age. He is in his 92nd year. It was the only thing that could be done."

Wednesday, October 28, 1891, began just as yesterday ended. The grey sky blanketed the fall colors, setting the tone for the day. The city had not yet come to life as William and Thurlow Strong traveled slowly along the quiet streets to the home of their father, George W. Strong. Helen was already there with her son, George, preparing Father for what would be his last journey. A quiet somber mood prevailed as the five family members left the Strong home and traveled slowly to the train station in downtown Monroe. Each of the men carried an overnight bag except for George W. Strong who packed a larger bag containing the last of his possessions. The once famous Captain Strong was leaving Monroe just as he arrived sixty years earlier with one travel bag. Unlike that earlier time when Monroe was known as Frenchtown, he was leaving without hope and unable to remember what he accomplished for the citizens that at one time depended on him.

A handful of family members were waiting at the station including Alonzo and Maria. For Alonzo, this was the end of a strained relationship he never understood. Helen, the oldest of the children, gave instructions to her son, George Diffenbaugh, to please make the trip to Kalamazoo, Michigan as comforting as possible for her father.

George W. Strong left Monroe with fleeting memories of a River, a shipping company, the railroad, a construction company, land and the Strong Hotel. He wondered where he was going but ceased to wonder before his questions were answered by his guardians.

It took the better part of a day with stops along the way to make the short trip to Kalamazoo. Mid-afternoon George Strong arrived at the insane asylum climaxing a journey that began 92 years earlier in young America. A short ride on horse and buggy took the men to the outskirts of the city and to the entrance of a massive complex.

Entrance to Asylum

Beyond the gate was the hospital that admitted its first patient in 1859. The patient population of the asylum had grown enough by 1874 to expand the complex and build a second large building.

A female wing was added a few years later. By 1891, the complex covered almost 250 acres with a number of buildings including a church. The complex had little effect on George W. Strong. Thurlow, William and the grandson were overwhelmed as they made their way to the admitting office. They were told the State Hospital was the country's first asylum to use "colonies." They were told that on a good day, George could use his skills in a farm-like setting. He

The Asylum Complex

could work and help provide food for the hospital. Each positive fact about the State Hospital was carefully explained in order to make the new patient at ease and the family comfortable with their decision. Thurlow and William encouraged their father to help with the gardening knowing there was little hope that at this stage in his life George W. Strong would be a productive citizen. The impressive complex and the concept of "colonies" began to ease the guilt associated with committing one's own father. The sons grasped at every constructive fact they were exposed to in order to ease the gravity of the situation with their struggling consciences.

They passed from one massive building to another and reminded their father that he knew a thing or two about large buildings. They

The Asylum Dining Room

recounted stories about the Union School and the Strong Hotel. George W. Strong could only reply that it was not the Park Hotel but the Strong Hotel. The fire came to his mind as he repeated the fire time and time again. They saw that Father was beginning to tire as they toured the dining room.

The day was nearing an end and there was one final building to visit. It housed the room that they knew would be their father's final resting place. They could not say those words to themselves or to each other.

It had worked out well. George W. Strong was too tired to collect coherent thoughts. His body told his mind it was time to lie down and it did not matter where. Where could be anywhere, just lie down. The farewells were but distant voices. He nodded, dozed nodded then dozed again and the beginning of a long and final sleep began.

William was the last to leave his father that day. The Strong Hotel was his home for many years resulting in a silent but closer

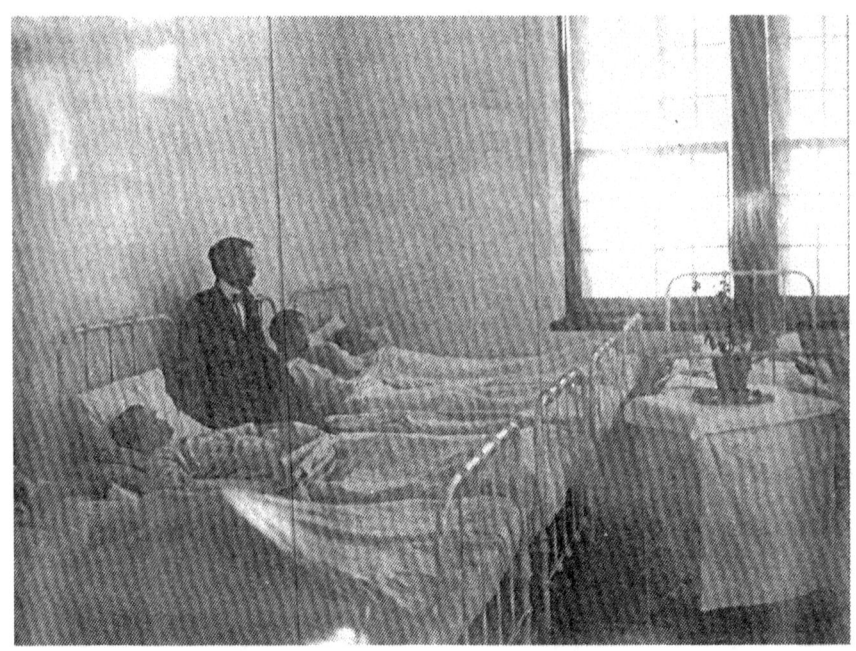
The Asylum Sleeping Room

relationship with the man who seemed larger than life at times. He said his final good-bye, wondering if a father knew his son or the son his father.

The family members returned to Monroe the next day leaving George W. Strong to face his final exile alone. There was an occasional sunny day in early November allowing Strong to experience an inner peace as the end neared. An endless winter followed as did cold dark days. The season and his illnesses wore down his will to live. George W. Strong began the process of dying when his mind began to fail and completed the journey to his end when his body followed.

Monroe Democrat **Thursday, March 3, 1892**
"The death of Capt. George W. Strong one of Monroe's oldest and most thorough citizens was announced Monday. His remains were brought from Kalamazoo Tuesday and funeral services held from the residence of his daughter Mrs. Diffenbaugh yesterday afternoon at 2'oclock, Rev. L. B. Bissell officiating. There was so much concerning

the life of Mr. Strong and so difficult to obtain that we have deferred referring to it until next week.

Monroe Democrat **Thursday, March 11, 1892**
"....He is survived by his sister, Mrs. Emma Bailey, of Adrian, who is in such precarious health that she has not yet been told of his death; four children, seventeen grandchildren and nine great grandchildren. He was reverentially borne to his well-earned rest by four of his grandchildren, George and Burnham Diffenbaugh, and Frank and Charles Strong."

After the service, the wooden coffin was placed on a horse drawn wagon and taken along Anderson Street (North Monroe) in route to Woodlawn Cemetery. Family and a small number of friends followed as they proceeded two short blocks to the corner of Elm and Monroe Streets. St. Mary's Church was to the west and as the family looked to the east they could see the Ilgenfritz home and the site of the Old Trading Post. They then crossed the wooden bridge over the River Raisin and proceeded along South Monroe Street. Just over the bridge to the east, they passed Beyer & Reisig Plumbers, then Bicking Groceries and Benno Jackson Jewelers. Across the street were Jacob Herman Groceries, Robert Balcom Dentist, George Kronbach Liquors and Jesse Dusseau Cigars. The Andereggs and Mrs. Donahue watched as the procession passed their homes on the following blocks. The family passed the Methodist and Episcopal churches and could look down the street and see the Union School which George helped build. Turning east on Fourth Street they passed Washington Street, the location of the Park Hotel and the home of Thurlow Strong on South Macomb Street. They continued east on Fourth Street passing the Boyd estate on their right and Navarre Street named after one of Monroe's first pioneer families. A few blocks farther were Jerome Street and the entrance to the cemetery. George W. Strong, many years earlier, had purchased one of the first plots on the west side of the cemetery entrance. It was large enough for the entire family and for the grandchildren. There he was laid to rest near his son, Captain Strong and son Thomas. Hannah was in a grave with a stone marked "Mother".

William Strong was next to follow his father in death on May 4, 1897. He was associated with the Strong Hotel and later the Park Hotel for many years. His wife preceded him in death by six years. His final years in ill health were spent with his sister, Helen, along with his son, on the corner of Noble and Anderson Streets. William Strong was buried in the family plot.

Alonzo died April 8, 1905, while residing at 257 Harrison Street. He had been in ill health for ten years. During his later years he had made his home at 257 Harrison Street with son Charles, who with his wife, made his last days happy and peaceful. He died fortified by the Last Sacraments of the Catholic Church that he attended for about two years. His burial service took place at St. Mary's Church Tuesday morning at 9:30. The Requiem Mass and sermon was given by Fr. Downey who returned from Dowagiac to be present at the funeral. Besides his son Charles, Mr. Strong left one daughter, Mrs. Elizabeth Trescott of Toledo, one brother Thurlow Strong of the City, and one sister, Mrs. Helen Diffenbaugh, also of Monroe. Alonzo Strong was the only member of the family not to be buried at Woodlawn Cemetery. He was buried at St. Joseph Catholic Cemetery.

Helen Diffenbaugh passed away December 2, 1909 at her home located at 258 First Street. Her husband, Christopher, passed away shortly after the Civil War. As years passed her growing infirmities curtailed her activities and overcame her in her later years. The funeral was held at the residence of her daughter, Mrs. Loose, with Rev. W. C. Burns officiating. She was buried in the Diffenbaugh plot next to the Strong plot at Woodland Cemetery.

Thurlow Strong was the last of the Strong Children to pass away at the age of 94. His death occurred on April 4, 1925, in his home at 217 South Macomb Street. He had suffered five attacks of pneumonia in his last twelve years but always managed to survive. Thurlow was an Officer of the Court for many years and Register of Deeds for six years after the Strong Hotel was sold. He was buried in the Strong family plot.

George W. Strong was one of the last of the pioneer builders of Old Monroe to pass away and ironically his was one of the first plots purchased at the entrance of the historic cemetery. His grave faces east to the rising sun in the morning. A rising star in one small town in one small part of a new land, he saw the greatness and opportunity that was America. The sunset was not as kind as the sunrise. A hero's life does not always entitle one to a hero's death as was the case for George W. Strong.

OZYMANDIAS

I met a traveller from an antique land
Who said: "Two vast and trunkless legs of stone
Stand in the desert. Near them on the sand
Half sunk, a shattered visage lies, whose frown
And wrinkled lip and sneer of cold command
Tell that its sculptor well those passions read
Which yet survive, stamped on these lifeless things,
The hand that mocked them and the heart that fed.
And on the pedestal these words appear:
"My name is Ozymandias, king of kings:
Look on my works, ye mighty, and despair!"
Nothing beside remains. Round the decay
Of that colossal wreck, boundless and bare,
The lone and level sands strech far away.

Percy Bysshe Shelley (1792-1822)

Historic Woodland Cemetery

Woodland Cemetery

Morton

Bulkley

Ilgenfritz

Wing

Smith

Toll

Humphrey

196

Noted Descendants of Elder John Strong

1731-1811 William Williams, revolutionary, signed Declaration
of Independence

1735-1825 John Adams, 2nd U.S. President

1738-1787 Ethan Allen, Revolutionary soldier

1745-1819 Caleb Strong, U.S. Senator and Governor

1750-1806 Henry Knox, 1st U.S. Sec, of War

1752-1817 Timothy Dwight (IV) President of Yale

1754-1807 Abraham Baldwin, U.S. Senator

1755-1776 Nathan Hale, Martyr spy American Revolution

1767-1848 John Quincy Adams, 6th U.S. President

1770-1840 John Kirkland, President of Harvard

1791-1872 Samuel Morse, Inventor of the Telegraph

1800-1891 George Bancroft, Secretary of the Navy

1800-1892 George W. Strong, Pioneer Builder of Monroe Mi.

1800-1868 Moses Beach, Co-founder of New York Sun

1800-1874 Millard Fillmore, 13th U.S. President

1809-1886 Frederick Barnard, President of Columbia University

1807-1882 Henry Wadsworth Longfellow, Poet

1809-1884 Cyrus McCormick, Farm Machinery

1811-1896 Harriet Beecher Stowe, Author

1820-1906 Susan B. Anthony, Suffragette

1822-1893 Rutheford B. Hayes, 19th U.S. President

1826-1885 George McClellan, Union General

1830-1886 Emily Dickinson, Poet

1832-1901 Philip E, Armour, Founder Armour Food

1834-1919 Henry Higginson, Founder of Boston Symphony

1837-1908 Grover Cleveland, 22 U.S. President

1837-1913 J. P. Morgan, Banker

1839-1937 J. D. Rockerfeller, Oil

The above are but a few of the descendants that can be found in the
following sources.

Dwight, Benjamin W. *Dwight's History of the Strong Family*,
Originally published, Albany, New York, 1871 - Reprinted,
Baltimore. Maryland 1975, 1984, 2000 Volume I & II

Roberts, Gary Boyd & Reitwiesner, William Addams *American
Ancestors and Cousins of the Princess of Wales* - Genealogical
Publishing Co., Inc Baltimore, 1985 Copyright 1984 by
Genealogical Publishing Co., Ind.

Peter,
You may find this interesting

PASSING OF A STRONG DESCENDANT

Many people are following the news of the death of Princess Diana but did you know that she was a Strong descendant? The following is a copy of Princess Diana's Strong lineage including Benjamin Dwight's ID number and page number.

Elder John Strong m. Abigail Ford {1–1,14}
Thomas Strong m. Rachel Holton{2–6,228} Jedediah Strong m. Freedom Woodward{2–8,769}
Joseph Strong m. Sarah Allen {3–4081,308} Preserved Strong m. Tabitha Lee {3–14273,986}
Joseph Strong Jr. {4–5735,330} m. Elizabeth Strong {4–18343,986}
Benajah Strong m. Lucy Bishop {5–6137,414}
Joseph Strong m. Rebecca Young {6–7193,414}
Eleanor Strong m. John Wood {7–7229,415}
Eleanor Wood m. Frank Work {8–7238,415}
Frances Eleanor Work m. James B. Burke Roche, 3rd Baron Fermoy {9–7240,415}
Edmund Maurice Burke Roche, 4th Baron Fermoy m. Ruth Sylvia Gill
Frances Ruth Burke Roche m. Edward John Spencer 8th Earl Spencer
Lady Diana Frances Spencer m. H.R.H. Charles Philip Arthur George, Prince of Wales

19

Vickey Strong
Jamestown, New York

Special thanks to Gary Boyd Roberts for permission to reprint information and for his willingness to shed light on his research.

The following pages 18 and 19 are taken directly from *American Ancestors and Cousins of the Princess of Wales.*

Roberts, Gary Boyd & Reitwiesner, William Addams *American Ancestors and Cousins of the Princess of Wales* - Genealogical Publishing Co., Inc Baltimore, 1985 Copyright 1984 by Genealogical Publishing Co., Ind.

ing descendants—again assuming thirteen generations, three now living, three children and thirty years per generation, and considerable cousin intermarriage. Thus the number of distant American kinsmen of anyone with sizable New England ancestry is enormous. Probably never, however, has it equalled more than half of the national population—because of extensive intermarriage and overlapping, which grow exponentially as the progenies of more immigrants are considered; because New Englanders by no means migrated everywhere; and because many Americans are totally of mid-Atlantic, southern, or nineteenth- or twentieth-century immigrant ancestry. Good statistical studies in genealogy are rare. As social historians explore these issues more exactly, many figures may change. However, as regards the probability of ancestry in common with the Princess of Wales for anyone with a considerable number of New England forebears, since the Princess has probably between twenty and thirty million New England-derived distant American relatives, as noted above, I should now estimate it as high as 20 or 25 percent.

However we attempt to calculate the likely *total* number of the Princess's New England-derived relatives, specific distant kinships to at least 250 of the several thousand most notable individuals in American history are clear. These 250, listed below with outlines of their descents from ancestors of Dr. Joseph Strong, include ten presidents or their wives (the two Adamses, Fillmore, Hayes, Cleveland, T. Roosevelt, Wilson, Coolidge, F. D. Roosevelt, and Truman); various "tycoon" families (Armours, Colts, Marshall Fields, Firestones, Fords, H. L. Hunts, McCormicks, J. P. Morgans, Potter Palmers, Pillsburys, C. W. Posts, Rockefellers, Scribners, Strauses, Tiffanys, Vanderbilts, and Whitneys); a sizable number of literary figures or their spouses, especially those leaders associated with Harvard, the mid-nineteenth-century "flowering of New England," abolition or reform (later Adamses, Alcotts, Beechers, Holmeses, Emerson, Longfellow, E. E. Hale, Bancroft, Prescott, Motley, T. D. Weld, Susan B. Anthony, and Elizabeth Cady Stanton); and numerous twentieth-century entertainment, media, or sports figures or their spouses (C. D. Gibson, Caruso, Valentino, Lillian and Dorothy Gish, John and Ethel Barrymore, Orson Welles, Humphrey Bogart, Spencer Tracy, Shirley Temple, Anthony Perkins, Julie Harris, Lee Remick, Dina Merrill, Sidney Lumet, Eddie Duchin, Henry Luce, Lowell Thomas, Edward R. Murrow, Ben Bradlee, George Gallup, the Alsops, Walter C. Camp, and "Gene" Tunney). Also included are five U.S. vice-presidents (Colfax, Morton, Sherman, Dawes, and Rockefeller), eight secretaries of state (Washburne, Root, Lansing, Stimson, Acheson, Dulles, Herter, and Vance), two presidents of Harvard (Kirkland and Lowell), seven presidents of Yale (Elisha Williams, the two Timothy Dwights, Woolsey, Hadley, Seymour, and Brewster), and a wide variety of twentieth-century literary figures (among others Frank Norris, L. F. Baum, Clarence Day, Hart Crane, F. Scott Fitzgerald, J. P.

Marquand, Robert Penn Warren, Archibald MacLeish, Barrett Wendell, Van Wyck Brooks, Samuel Eliot Morison, Arthur Schlesinger, Jr., and Erle Stanley Gardner, or their wives). So inclusive, these 250 seem a fair sample of the Yankee, and especially Connecticut and Connecticut Valley Yankee, contribution to American history. Involved in both the Revolution and the formation of the Federalist mercantile elite of Salem and Boston, whose second generation was in large part responsible for "the flowering of New England," Unitarianism, abolitionism, and early feminism, these notable kinsmen of Dr. Joseph Strong and their immediate forebears also moved, as did he and his children and grandchildren, to New York City and/or the Midwest. There they helped to found both the industrial oligarchy of the immediate post-Civil War decades, and its own second generation offspring, inter-city turn-of-the-century "society," headed by the 400 in New York. A few less wealthy but locally notable kinsmen produced political leaders, especially in upstate New York and Ohio. In this century "society" settled into an "eastern establishment" much represented by these 250 (note the just-listed secretaries of state); literature and the arts and sciences have continued to expand and flower, both within and outside New England and its colleges; and much business opportunity has moved to the South or the West (note the California-based entertainment and media figures above). Unfortunately, space considerations preclude documenting each generation in the descents of these 250 notable figures from various ancestors of Dr. Joseph Strong. One major source has been my own research, including various pamphlets and "The Mowbray Connection" (23 volumes, manuscript collection at NEHGS and elsewhere, for some discussion of which see *The Connecticut Nutmegger*, 10 [1977]: 3-12, and *The Detroit Society for Genealogical Research Magazine*, 41 [1978]: 141; 42 [1979]: 191), collected and compiled since 1966. All descents outlined below have been rechecked, however, and much additional research undertaken as well.

The remainder of this chapter consists of (1) a detailed genealogical summary of the seven generations between Dr. Joseph Strong and the Princess of Wales; (2) an ancestor table of Dr. Strong, again covering seven generations; and (3) the list of 250 notable figures who share part of his New England ancestry, together with an outline of the generations between each of the 250 and every nearest common forebear. Before proceeding to this specific data and documentation, however, I wish to acknowledge several colleagues, partial sponsors, and individuals or media who have encouraged this research into the American and New England ancestry of the Princess of Wales. First among my colleagues, who exhausted sources at the Library of Congress and the National Archives, and undertook research with me in Chillicothe, is William Addams Reitwiesner of Silver Spring, Maryland, whose monograph, "The American Ancestors and Relatives of Lady Diana Frances Spencer," was sent to various scholars and libraries in the spring of 1981 and is incor-

Acknowledgments

Karen McLaughlin (Alonzo Strong)
Monroe, Michigan

Patrick Meehan   (Thomas Strong)
Pe Ell, Wa.

Jarvis Strong (founder of Assoc)
Reston Va.

Robert Sheldon Strong
Mason, Mi

Lyle Strong
Swartz Creek Mi. 48473

Vickey Strong
Jamestown, New York

Dear Peter,

I will be happy to share with you whatever information I have. Are you also a descendent of G. W. Strong? I've wanted to travel to Monroe, MI someday, but I live in SW Washington State. Work and the fact that two of my grown children live in the Phoenix, AZ area limit my travel in time and scope to the West and Southwest. Hopefully, when I retire I will be able to take more extended trips.

G. W. Strong would be my great grandfather, with my descent through Thomas Tufts Strong. My grandmother, was Lillian Lucille Strong. Family tradition has it that the twins served in the Civil

War. In fact, one of them (I'm not sure which one) apparently feel asleep on guard duty, court-martialed, and given a sentence of death. As the story goes, his mother traveled to Washington, D. C. and was able to arrange a meeting with President Lincoln to plead for a pardon. The pardon was granted, and my mother, as a young girl, wore the same dress her grandmother had worn to visit President Lincoln in a parade at the Montana State Centennial. Someone else asked me about how Alonzo's marriage was received by his family. I really don't know anything about this, however if it caused a big scandal I think I would have heard. The interesting thing is that my grandmother, Lillian Lucille (Strong) Cowan, Converted to Catholicism as a adult after suffering a serious illness and being treated in a Catholic hospital. When she married my grandfather, Robert Benjamin Cowan, she insisted that he convert before she would marry him. All their children were all raised a Catholic.

Thomas Tufts Strong was about 25 years older than his wife, and he died in 1891 at age 63. At sometime after that, Great Grandmother Strong moved with the children to Indianapolis, IN where she had family. That is where the children were raised. Throughout the years since, there have been several migrations westward.

To the best of my knowledge, this Strong family is descended from Elder John Strong to Massachusetts between 1630 and 1635 for religious reasons. I can share that information with you if you wish, however I have not researched it carefully and have no documents prior to the G. W. Strong family. I do have some postcards of the hotel dating from the 1920's when family members from back in Monroe east traveled I have a photograph to Thomas Tufts Strong taken in Monroe, MI. You can view it at my web page at <http://www2.localaccess.com/meehan>. You will find it under the section "Old Photos" along with photos of my grandmother, her sisters, and one of her brothers. I will attach here a family group sheet for the Thomas Tufts family:

Misc. family Notes: In the 1850 Census, Thomas' occupation was listed as a sailor. One assumes that he worked for his older brother George A. Strong whose occupation was listed as Steamboat Captain.

Family moved to the United States when Wilhelminna was five years old, or about 1857. Family name was changed to Sherman when they moved to the United States.

F. Patrick Meehan

I hadn't heard any information passed down in the family regarding George W. Strong's death. It certainly sounds like an unfortunate end for a man who did a great deal as an American pioneer. I would be interested to know what you are able to find out about the possible causes of condition.

Here is what I have on George W. Strong's descent from Elder John Strong. One caveat however, I haven't personally researched all the connections, and therefore I can't personally attest to this line of descent. Most of the information I have preceding George W. Strong was derived from information shared on the Strong Family Web page and from email correspondence with others researching this family. More conclusive results would have to be derived from intensive research into wills, land records, marriage & baptismal records where available, etc. Anyway, here is what I have: I will include information on the George W. Strong family as I know it. It is interesting to note the path of migration westward by noting places of birth for George W. and Hanna Strong, the place of their marriage, and the places of birth for each of children.

F. Patrick Meehan   meehan@localaccess.com

I hope this information helps in your efforts.

Five generations ago, George W. Strong came to Monroe, Michigan. He worked hard, established himself in the community and raised his family. I am a descendent of George W. Strong. My lineage in the Strong Family follows from George to Alonzo to Charles to Carl to Arlene (Strong) Weaver, my mother.

I believe that our family today is living under the blessings sowed by George W. Strong, Alonzo and so on. From the research we know that hard work and religion were a huge part of my ancestors' lives. Preferences seemed to fluctuate from generation to generation between the Methodist and Catholic religions. However, church was always an integral part of their lives.

I have been very curious to know why there is a noticeable lack of historical information concerning Alonzo, my great, great grandfather. Perhaps a "falling out" occurred when Alonzo, raised in the Methodist home of George and Hannah, married an Irish Catholic, Maria Quinn. This could have been a sign of the prejudice of the times.

I am grateful to have the opportunity to say a word about my family in this book.

Karen McLaughlin

Monroe County Library System
Ellis Reference and Information Center
Carl Katafiasz
Charmaine Wawrzyniec

Monroe County Historical Commission
Chris Kull - Archivist
Lynn Reaume

Glastonbury Ct. Hartford County Museum
Glastonbury Ct.

Historical Library at Glastonbury
Phyllis Reed

CT. Genealogy

Ray Dushane (Register of Deeds and newspaper research)
Monroe, Michigan

Newspaper Publications in Historic Old Monroe
The Monroe Sentinel 1823 - 1836
The Monroe Times 1836 - 1837
The Monroe Gazette 1841
The Monroe Advocate 1841 - 1845
The Monroe Commercial 1849 - 1885
The Monroe Democrat Weekly 1883 - 1898
The Monroe Democrat 1898 - 1911
The Record Commercial 1908 - 1911
The Monroe News Courier 1915 - 1917
Name changed to *The Monroe Evening News* in 1918

Produced by The Monroe Publishing Co.

Wars during the lifetime of
George W. Strong

A number of local wars took place during the time spent in Michigan. It is interesting to note these events since they impacted the lives of the pioneers living at the time. A brief source for this information can be found on the internet on the following site:

"http://www.michigan.gov/dmva/0,1607,7-126-2360_3003_3009-16956--,00.html"
Following the Toledo War and statehood, a band of US citizens attempted to gain control of part of Canada, then under British control.

www.michigan.gov/dmva/0,1607,7-126-2360_3003_3009-16956--,00.html - 29k - "http://64.233.167.104/search?q=cache:EPhCsEXxxQ0J:www.michigan.gov/dmva/0,1607,7-126-2360_3003_3009-16956--,00.html+patriot+war&hl=en" - "/search?hl=en&lr=&q=related:www.michigan.gov/dmva/0,1607,7-126-2360_3003_3009-16956--,00.html"

The Toledo War

Contact: paocmn@michigan.gov

The Northwest Ordinance of 1787 established an east-west line drawn from the southern tip of Lake Michigan across the base of the peninsula. The original line was drawn using maps that showed the line intersecting Lake Erie north of the Maumee River. This is the territorial "line-of- scrimmage" that Ohioans recognized when their constitution was drafted in 1803. When the Michigan Territory was created in 1805, surveyors realized the tip of Lake Michigan was actually further south and included the area that would later become Toledo.

This revelation had the Ohioans in Congress screaming, "Offsides!" They immediately campaigned to have the northern line accepted as the official border. In 1817, U.S. Surveyor General, and former Ohio governor, Edward Tiffin, sent William Harris out to survey the line according to Ohio's constitution. The Michigan Territorial Governor, Lewis Cass, went to President James Monroe to protest the call. John A. Fulton was called into the fray to make another survey of the disputed claim in accordance with the Northwest Ordinance.

It was not surprising that the two surveys resulted in two lines eight miles apart at Lake Erie and five miles apart at the Indiana border, with a total of 468 square miles in between. Although Ohio still claimed the Toledo Strip as its own, the squabbling momentarily ceased and Michigan quietly assumed jurisdiction over the area.

The controversy heated up again when Michigan sought admission to the union on December 11, 1833. In spite of Michigan's presence in the Toledo Strip, Ohio Congressmen successfully lobbied to block Michigan's acceptance as a state until it agreed to Ohio's version of the boundary. Massachusetts Representative, and former President, John Quincy Adams, supported Michigan saying, "Never in the course of my life have I known a controversy of which all the right so clearly on one side and all the power so overwhelmingly on the other."

Ohio's position was so strong that Governor Robert Lucas refused to negotiate with Michigan over the issue. Michigan's territorial council countered by passing a resolution that would impose heavy fines on anyone other than Michigan or federal officers trying to exercise jurisdiction in the Toledo Strip. In a blatant act of defiance, Governor Lucas turned the disputed region into a county named after himself and appointed a sheriff and judge. Michigan's "boy governor" had had enough! Stevens T. Mason mobilized his troops and headed towards Ohio. The Toledo War had begun.

The War involved more saber-rattling and up-one-manship than it did shooting and blood-letting. For instance, after the Ohio legislature voted to approve a $300,000 military budget, Michigan upped the ante by approving one with $315,000. Michigan's militia did end up arresting some Ohio officials, capturing nine surveyors, and firing a few shots over the heads of others as they ran out of the area. But only Ohio inflicted any casaulties, when a buckeye name Two Stickney stabbed a Michigan Sheriff during a tavern brawl.

When President Andrew Jackson stepped in, the war ended. Jackson removed Mason from office and the militia commander, General Joseph W. Brown disbanded his troops. But Congress still held Michigan statehood hostage until it agreed to Ohio's claims. The citizens of Michigan set up a state government anyway, and elected Stevens T. Mason governor.

Michigan eventually became the 26th state of the union, on the 26th of January, 1837. But its territory did not include the Toledo Strip. Instead, it gained title to the western three-quarters of the upper peninsula as compensation; 9,000 square miles of the most valuable timber, iron, and copper country in America.

Like so many of the gridiron battles that continue to rage today, a game isn't decided on one play, but a series of plays. Poor officiating may have taken Michigan officially out of the campaign for the Toledo Strip, but in retrospect, it's obvious who won the War.

The Patriot War

Immediately following the "Toledo War," Michigan became a state on January 26, 1837. A year later, January 1838, the militia, under the state organization, was in active operations during the "Patriot War." Although it was not a major campaign, this war did furnish some action for the soldiers.

The "Patriot War' was brought about by some residents of both upper Canada and the United States, of Irish descent or birth, and United States citizens who had moved to Canada. These "Patriots," as they called themselves, planned to detach the peninsula lying between the Michigan frontier and the Niagara frontier from Canada and attach it to the United States. Their base of operations was located in Michigan and they were organized into secret groups known as

"Hunters Lodges."

The points of assembly were Fort Gratiot (Port Huron), Mount Clemens, Detroit, and Gibralter. Meetings were called, secret military organizations created, and Dr. E.A. Theller, an Irish enthusiast for anything opposed to Great Britain, committed some overt acts for which he was arrested, tried, convicted, and sentenced to the citadel of Quebec; he later escaped and fled to Detroit.

In the early winter of 1837-38, straggling parties of armed men waited along the border for the ice to form on the St. Clair river. This was the route over which they planned to enter Canada, unfurl their flag, and establish a temporary government in rebellion against the British crown. They attempted to seize Fort Gratiot, but were foiled by a detachment of the (1,1607,7-126-2360_3003_3009-16972--.00.html). Their arms and ammunition were taken to Detroit.

In the latter part of December 1837, the "Patriots" used a small steamboat to cross into Canada and landed a short distance above Windsor. They marched down to the village opposite Detroit and in the engagement that followed--the Battle of Windsor--a number of men on both sides were killed and wounded. The "Patriots" scattered to the woods.

A plot was then discovered to capture the United States Arsenal at Dearborn and take possession of the arms stored there. To thwart this action, a company of the Michigan Militia was assigned guard duty at the arsenal. The excitement continued through 1838, however the "Battle of Windsor" is considered the closing of the war.

During its fourth session in 1839, the state legislature enacted legislation that provided more effective defense for the state. This action, most likely inspired by the frontier troubles during the "Patriot War," provided for the organization of a brigade of "State Guards." These troops were to be a sort of superior militia and were to have the preference in the distribution of arms and accoutrements.

Michigan Answers the Call to Arms in the Civil War

The surrender of Fort Sumter on April 15, 1861, was startling news throughout the country, and Michigan soon received the President's call for volunteers. The state was asked to furnish one regiment of infantry fully armed, clothed, and equipped to aid the federal government in suppressing the rebellion. Although the state treasury was not in a condition to meet this request, subscription made the necessary amount available; ten companies were at once mobilized.

The President's call for Michigan troops was promptly met by the mustering in of the First Regiment and its early movement to the seat of war in Virginia. In the meantime, the War Department authorized Michigan to raise three other regiments, but at the same time stated that it was "important to reduce rather than increase that number." This authority only covered the Second, Third, and Fourth Infantry Regiment, already in process of recruitment. Many companies throughout the state, not included in the regiments named above, recruited without authority in the hope of obtaining places in those or other regiments. They were disappointed however, and 13 companies found service in the units of other states. By December 1861, Michigan had sent 13 infantry regiments, three cavalry regiments, and five batteries of light artillery, totaling 16,475 officers and enlisted men to the front.

As The War Continues

On July 2, 1862, the War Department assigned Michigan a quota of 11,686, as part of the proclamation for 500,000 men. The regiments recruited were as follows: 21st, Ionia; 22nd, Pontiac; 23rd, East Saginaw; and 24th, from Detroit and Wayne county. More companies were raised than could be placed in the district regiments, so the 25th (Kalamazoo) and the 26th (Jackson) infantry regiments were formed and sent into the field. The Fourth, Fifth, and Sixth Cavalry regiments were also organized.

Following the expiration of their three-year enlistment periods at the beginning of 1864, five thousand five hundred forty-five veterans reenlisted, entitling the units in which they were serving to the designation of "Veteran." These organizations were the First, Second, and Third Cavalry; Second, Fifth, Eighth, Ninth, l0th, 12th, 13th, 14th, 15th, and 16th Regiments of Infantry; the Sixth Heavy Artillery (formerly the Sixth Infantry) and Batteries B, C, and E, First Light Artillery.

Because Michigan was on the Canadian border, it was continually threatened with invasion by rebels who had found refuge in Canada and were encouraged by the Confederate government to raid the northern states. During the time of these threatened raids, Michigan relied on the following forces to defend its borders against any hostile demonstration: six companies of the Second Regiment Veteran Reserve Corps, three companies of the State Troops, the Scott Guard, Detroit Light Guard, and Lyon Guard, with a section of light artillery.

At the close of the Civil War, Michigan's Colonel Benjamin Pritchard and the 4th Michigan Cavalry captured Jefferson Davis, the defeated Confederate President.

Michigan's Contribution

From April 1861 to April 1865, Michigan furnished 90,747 men, not counting 1,982 men commuting and 4,000 Michigan men who served in the units of other states. The first Michigan troops discharged from federal service, the 20th Regiment of Infantry, arrived in the state from the battle field on June 4, 1865 and the last, the Third and Fourth Infantry, arrived on June 10, 1866.

War with Mexico

On May 19, 1846, following the initial battle between Mexican forces and United States troops under Gen. Zachary Taylor in the disputed territory between the Neuces and Rio Grande rivers,

Michigan's Governor received a request from the War Department to enroll a regiment of volunteer infantry. Made up of 10 companies, the regiment would be held in readiness for service until called for by the President.

Under the first call, 13 independent companies, 11 infantry and two cavalry, responded. However, only Detroit's (1,1607,7-126-2360_3003_3009-16972--,00.html) were accepted. The men were sent to garrison the posts at Mackinac and Sault Ste. Marie to free the regular troops stationed there for duty in Mexico. Of the companies tendered for service, four were from Detroit, two from Monroe, three from Lenawee County, and one each came from St. Clair, Hillsdale, Berrien, and Wayne County (outside Detroit).

The First Michigan Volunteers was enrolled and mustered in answer to a second call in October 1847. The companies were from: Kalamazoo, St. Clair and Wayne Counties, Pontiac, three from Detroit, western Michigan, Hillsdale, Lenawee, Monroe, Marshall, and the southeastern part of the state. The companies were mustered into federal service at various times during November and December 1847 and January and February 1848.

Prior to January 1848, six companies were sent to the battle area and landed at Vera Cruz, Mexico, where the four remaining Michigan companies later joined them. General Scott was already occupying Mexico City when the last companies advanced as far as Cordova, which they garrisoned until the peace treaty was signed. Michigan troops guarded General Scott's communications lines.
Although Michigan men were in the field for nearly six months, they never saw battle. The regiment was mustered out at Detroit on July 23, 1848.

The Spanish-American War

Michigan Joins the War

The Spanish-American War is assumed to have started April 21, 1898. On April 23, the President called for 125,000 volunteers. A second call was made May 25 for another 75,000 men. The call was at first confined to existing units but was then issued to the citizens at large. Members of existing units were the first to be accepted and organized.

Michigan's Governor ordered out the National Guard and attempted to turn the units over intact as volunteers to the federal government. This however, was not in compliance with federal law and as a result, each individual was required to volunteer as an individual rather than as part of a unit.

Practically every member of the National Guard volunteered. They were reorganized into the same units in which they had been serving but the regiments were reorganized so that the existing five regiments of eight companies each became four regiments of 12 companies each. To fill the regiments, eight new companies had to be organized. Each Michigan regiment was to contain 1,000 men. Upon the second call, Michigan furnished one more regiment of 1,200 men as well as an additional 200 men to each of the four original regiments.

The regiments organized in the spring of 1898 were designated the 31st, 32nd, 33rd, and 34th Michigan Volunteer Infantry, following in numerical order the infantry regiments of the Civil War. They were all mobilized at Island Lake, near Detroit.

The 31st was mustered May 11 and left on May 15 for Chickamauga Park, Ga. The 32nd was mustered May 14 and left May 19 for Tampa, Fla. The 33rd was mustered May 20 and left May 28 for Camp Alger, near Washington, D.C. The 34th was mustered May 25 and left June 6 for Camp Alger. Under the second call of the President, the 35th was organized and left for Camp Meade, Pa. September 14.

The Real Enemy is Disease

The men in the southern camps, particularly at Chickamauga and Camp Alger, suffered severely from sickness. At Chickamauga, there was an epidemic of typhoid fever, and the 31st Regiment moved to Knoxville, Tenn. where it remained until

January 25, 1899, when it was sent to Cuba.

The 31st landed at Cienfugas and was then distributed in the towns of Santa Clara Province to preserve order and protect property. The regiment performed guard duty until it returned to the United States April 25, 1899. It was disbanded at Savannah, Ga. on May 17, 1899. While in service, 20 men died from sickness in southern camps and hospitals.

The 32nd was one of the earliest regiments moved to Fernandian, Fla., where it remained in camp for some time. It was among those assigned to service in Cuba but did not leave the United States. While enroute, its transport ship collided with another ship. The regiment was unloaded; it never left the port. After remaining in Florida for awhile, the regiment was transferred to Fort McPherson, Ga., where it remained until September. It then returned to Michigan and was disbanded between October 25 and November 9, 1898. While in service, 20 men from this regiment also died of disease.

June 10, 1910

President Taft

Custer Dedication – June 4, 1910

Hotel in 1934

SATISFACTION

—for you! Good food, excellent service, congenial atmosphere . . . all at acceptable prices!

Club Breakfasts . . 25c 35c 50c
Served from 7 to 10 A. M.
Dinner   75c
Served 11:30 A. M. to 2 P. M.
Evening Meal   75c
Served 5.30 to 8 P. M.
Special Sunday Dinner . $1.50
Served 12 to 3:30 & 5:30 to 7:30 P. M.

M. E. N.   3-17-44

THE PARK HOTEL

C. B. Southworth, Owner and Operator for 51 Years

SUNDAY DINNER

May 31, 12 to 2:30 P. M.

MENU

FRUIT CUP OR TOMATO JUICE
CREAM OF ASPARAGUS
COMBINATION SALAD

CHOICE OF
FRIED SPRING CHICKEN WITH CREAM GRAVY
BROILED PORTERHOUSE STEAK
BAKED HAM WITH SWEET POTATOES

BOILED OR MASHED POTATOES
GREEN STRING BEANS—DICED CARROTS
PARK HOTEL BISCUITS

APPLE PIE—STRAWBERRY SHORTCAKE
VANILLA ICE CREAM AND CAKE
CHEESE AND WAFERS—COFFEE

Our Dining Room Is Closed Saturdays

THE PARK HOTEL

C. B. Southworth, owner and operator for 49 years.

The Park Hotel Closes
December 18, 1962

Demolition of Hotel built by George W. Strong in 1868

December 18, 1962

www.ingramcontent.com/pod-product-compliance
Lightning Source LLC
Chambersburg PA
CBHW061353280526
45784CB00001B/236